THE
MILWAUKEE
ANTHOLOGY

MORE CITY ANTHOLOGIES BY BELT

Under Purple Skies: The Minneapolis Anthology

St. Louis Anthology

The Akron Anthology

Right Here, Right Now: The Buffalo Anthology

Rust Belt Chicago: An Anthology

The Cincinnati Anthology

The Cleveland Anthology

A Detroit Anthology

Happy Anyway: A Flint Anthology

Grand Rapids Grassroots: An Anthology

The Pittsburgh Anthology

Car Bombs to Cookie Tables: The Youngstown Anthology

THE
MILWAUKEE
ANTHOLOGY

Edited by Justin Kern

First Edition 2019
ISBN: 978-1948742382

Belt Publishing
3143 W. 33rd Street, Cleveland, Ohio 44109
www.beltpublishing.com

Book design by Meredith Pangrace
Cover by Paloma Chavez

"The truth begins with us. Instead of passing each other like ships in the night, we must fight until our truths stretch to the ends of the world."

–Sandra Parks

contents

contents

IN PERSON

STATE OF THE ARTS

OUT THERE

contents

INTRODUCTION
(A.K.A. "THAT'S THEIR HARD TIME")

Milwaukee is a living caveat, half an asterisk exploding westward from Lake Michigan, tendrils pointed at but not reaching college/capitol daydream Madison, metropolis Chicago, and all that Iowa mental landscape in between. It's a city that's overly proud of itself and too often overlooked for its greatness. Exceptional in its trauma and celebration, except when the business of daily life gets gloriously in the way. At a recent peak and hitting new lows. It's a big town and small city, run down and redeveloped, tararrel and terror.

I could fill the Deep Tunnel with similar summarizing intros I've attempted: scribbled Post-Its from an afternoon split between the Heal the Hood block party and the very public christening of the slick new Milwaukee Bucks arena; wispy visions during bicycle rides to Mamie's or Holy Land Bakery or Kaszube's Park or band practice in a garage in St. Francis; laptop keyboard stabs while peeking out of frost-crystalized bedroom office windows during zero-degree weeks; dialogue I assumed sounded smart as I pointed downtown from Riverwest while showing off to my dad's visiting biker buddies or in a nod from a car window while driving the whole of Twenty-seventh Street with my artsy college friends . . .

Thankfully, the massive talent accumulated in this anthology does all of the hard, creative work I could've dreamed for in expressing dynamic, distinct viewpoints of Milwaukee. The subsequent roster of writers and voices gives you the lesser-heard, silent, and necessary stories from our city, above the din of one perspective, over the fray of culture too dominated by the loudest outrage or the simplest take. It's not every story; it couldn't be. But in a city too often dominated by its separations, here's a shot at coming together. To show a place that's more than its trivialities, in ways that are probably the same or weirder than wherever you're at. Here is Milwaukee today—some, but not the sum—as the Cream City of tomorrow hopefully, painfully makes its way.

— **Justin Kern, editor**
October 2018

EVERY DAY

About Leaving

DASHA KELLY

I only think of leaving you
in between the slotted points
of morning
Before swinging my feet
from beneath these worn blankets
and forcing my weight
onto the floor
I think of leaving you then
Imagining myself rising to greet
the sun from some
new horizon
a new mattress
a new walk to brush my teeth
I think of leaving you
behind me
then
Tucking away your disappointments
and afflictions
like snapshots
stuffed into shoe boxes
never destined for a frame
We'd always talk
about sorting them out and
pressing labels onto
photo album spines, but
supposing
is all we've ever been good at
Together, wondering what this relationship
might be if I could reengineer
the ambitious wiring that led me back
to you in the first place
If you could engine past the rust
and biting decay I

once said gave you
your charm

Infatuation and foresight are not meant to
swirl inside the same thought

I'm sure we never planned on
resenting each other
for the edges of these blueprints
we've worked so diligently to align
I wouldn't be surprised if you hoped
to find a note one day
An overwritten apology
scratched in my lopsided and tumbling hand
You might not even
read it right away
Breathe aloud that sigh of relief trapped
behind your cream city bricks
Lie back instead letting dry stubble,
aluminum cans, and refuse
consume you
Remind yourself that there are others
who will love you just the way you are
Adoring hearts plentiful who won't insist on
constant evolution
studying the neighboring Joneses
or changing the only way
you ever learned how to love:
Conditionally
and without flourish

And I always knew this about you
Didn't settle myself into your spaces
unaware of your history
unsympathetic to the rugged hands that
yanked and pulled at your upbringing
tragically convincing you that
this
is all you should ever strive for

And you knew that I've always been different
Not necessarily special or extraordinary
just different
That I've only been coached to peek under the sun
for promise and wild imaginings
You've been more successful at being practical
You know better, you said, than to risk singeing
the tips of your fingers on the surface of the sun
I tried to show you how
beautiful the scars can be sometimes

I suppose we're both guilty
of waiting
of secretly hoping for more, of looking
for some folding back of rigid demands
and a chiseling away of sharp corners
We've each tried our hands at changing in some previous lifetime
You, failing to model your trendy peers
Me, bumbling through my revised declarations of independence
We've long ago resigned ourselves to be ourselves
So how can this sense of "we" survive
the harsh lights of failed expectations?

I empty my coffee into the sink
I slide on my shoes and my lipstick
and prepare to wrap
my face in
raw morning sun
I won't think of
leaving you then
With your crisp smell
slipping familiar into my chest
Your concrete rising to meet my feet
You've always known how I move, even
when you couldn't understand my walk
I don't plan to leave you
anytime soon, Milwaukee

I'm still hopeful
we can find more loving to do

Gunshots and Carrots

LAURA RICHARD MARSHALL

Sage appeared in my doorway, wrapped in her comforter, her big sister right behind her. "Mom, were those gunshots?"

It was 9:30 p.m. and the girls had been in bed for an hour. I had heard the shots—three of them with several eerie pauses between—fired in the alley behind my house. I was hoping that the girls were asleep and didn't hear. But here we were on my bed having a conversation I wasn't prepared to have tonight. "Mom, why do we live in Sherman Park?"

We've lived here ten years now and these conversations are never easy, especially now that my kids are older. I talked with my girls for a while that night, which put me in a strange sisterhood of mothers who have had detailed discussions with their children about what to do when we hear nearby gunshots.

I called 911 and they sent a squad car. The officers in the squad called to tell me they were in the area. The girls slept in bed with me for a while that night, and as they drifted to sleep, I felt the same doubt and fear that my sisterhood likely feels: Am I able to protect my children? Is this the best place for us? Should we move?

Now I'm reminded, as I often am, that the ability to ask these questions is a privilege. The ability to move elsewhere is a privilege. I know that there are mothers who don't have the resources to consider these options. And knowing that humbles me.

The next morning, my alarm went off at 5:10 a.m. I had planned to meet some neighbors to go for a run at the Washington High School track. I jogged over to the school, feeling miserable in the cold dark morning because of the night before, but also because I am not particularly fond of running. But running seemed to be a logical next step in becoming a good adult person, so I had agreed to meet them.

I arrived at the track the same time as the Walking Ladies, a group of older black women who apparently met each morning to walk the track together. They were obviously morning people, calling good morning to me and each other in the dark. My neighbors and I began our run and I realized very quickly that my companions were people who actually enjoyed running. They were not people like me who only enjoyed thinking they liked to run. With each lap around the track, I begin to grasp this irreconcilable difference. Each time we ran past the Walking Ladies on the track, one of them sang for us, encouraged us, or did something else really kind. And then I felt profound joy that I lived here, and believed that everyone in Milwaukee should consider Sherman Park as a place to live because a neighborhood just doesn't get any better than this.

But then I got kinda mad about the whole thing because I wished Sherman Park would just stop dangling the carrot in front of me. I wished this neighborhood would just make up its mind: either be the hood or be Urban Mayberry. Sherman Park could be peaceful and all Mayberry-ish for months on end and the day that my mother came to town, someone would decide to light a car on fire, or smash into someone's car and drive away. As a result, my mother now has a rather skewed opinion of my neighborhood. Sherman Park, could you just keep it together when my mom comes to town? Thanks.

That day, I felt mostly discouraged. I checked the news to see if there was any report about the gunshots the night before and found nothing, which was a relief, but it made me wonder why someone was shooting in the alley. What were they shooting at? I'll never know.

When I picked up the girls from school that day, I decided to take them to Atwater Park in the calm oasis of Shorewood. Yes, shiny clean Shorewood is what I needed that day. I took Capitol Drive and the traffic was slow-going. As we approached the park, I could see why the traffic had been slow: two cars collided and one of them careened off the road into Atwater Park and came to a halt very near the playground equipment. All the moms had gathered their kids and thankfully, no one had been hurt.

There's so much irony there that I have to laugh. Man, get it together Shorewood. Y'all got some problems.

So these past few weeks, I've been feeling like there's a tight rubber band of anxiety in my chest. I've begun to wonder if anyone can live in a place like

Sherman Park without developing some kind of anxiety disorder. Recently, I was invited to a cabin up north with friends and it was therapy for my soul. We ate good food together, read books, sat by the fire and laughed, and I heard a story that helped me process some of my anxiety.

The cabin we stayed at has been in my friend's family since the early 1900s and in the living room is an old wood table. As the story goes, a group of friends were playing poker around this table when the fireplace ignited a fire that ended up burning the whole cabin to the ground. The friends were able to save the table by throwing it out the window and carrying it to a neighboring cabin. In fact, this table was the only thing they were able to save from the fire. When they got to the neighbor's house, there was nothing more they could do about the fire, so they gathered around the table and finished their poker game. The cabin was eventually rebuilt and today it proudly houses that old poker table.

It's a crazy story and hard to know how much of it has been embellished through the years, but I dig it. Here's how that story helped me: those friends had a legit crisis on their hands, they saved what they could, and went to their neighbors. I suppose that story reminded me of Sherman Park—when things get hard, we know we have each other.

So what is Sherman Park? Is it the hood or is it Urban Mayberry?

I don't think either description fits. I think this neighborhood is more like art, in progress. And the people who live here are artists, responding honestly to the underbelly we've seen and creating a culture that is beautiful, honest, and worthy. It's art that sounds a lot like voices singing out encouragement to each other in the early morning hours.

Most of us have been here too long to be angry activists with simple answers to complex, generations-old questions. Instead, we're doing the time-consuming and tedious work of being reconciled with each other. We're going to save what we can and rebuild as best we can. We know it's going to be hard and beautiful. All the best things are.

My Own Private Mary Nohl House

CRIS SIQUEIRA

In the suburb of Fox Point, just north of Milwaukee proper, the house where artist Mary Nohl once lived is surrounded by concrete sculptures and embellished inside and out with stunningly detailed artwork. Nohl was a recluse in her later years and rumored to be a witch, a reputation she was apparently amused by, as one of her front steps is decorated with pebbles that spell out the word "boo."

Mary Nohl died in 2001, the year I first visited Milwaukee. I came to see my friend Carolina, who had moved here from our native city of São Paulo. She was a film graduate student at UW-Milwaukee and part of a vibrant artistic community. I met talented, creative, and inspired people. I fell in love with the impossibly huge Lake Michigan and the eerily quiet streets of the East Side. Milwaukee was like an antidote to the chaos and violence of the hyper-industrial megalopolis where I grew up. The type of place where a person could settle down and live peacefully in a house surrounded by art. In 2004, I applied and was accepted to the same program as Carolina. Carolina left Wisconsin never to return two weeks after I arrived.

One thing I didn't know about Milwaukee is that people tend to leave it. The people I made a soul connection with, the eccentric and artistic types, they're gone before you can say, "But what about Darling Hall?" They go to California or the East Coast chasing jobs, or recognition, or both. They move to Portland, Asheville, Austin, or Seattle, looking for diversity, or like-minded liberals, or legal pot. A couple of friends moved to Savannah because who wouldn't? They all look happy and prosperous on social media, and sometimes I envy them. I would have left Milwaukee, too, if I thought straight about money.

I still work as a corporate translator for Brazilian branches of multinational companies. What was a side job for most of my life has become my only source of income. Making money in Brazil and spending it in the United States is not super smart. As of this writing, one US dollar is worth four Brazilian reais, which means I earn twenty-five cents to the dollar. I know, ouch. Most immigrants do the exact opposite: they make money here where the currency is strong to support their families back home. Of course, the right thing to do would be to get a job in Milwaukee. I've tried, so hard. I've applied for positions where I've been under qualified, over qualified, and just right, but never a fit. I've tried anything that seemed even remotely appealing. When I wasn't called back for interviews, I went to a career coach to adjust my resume. The main takeaway from those sessions was that it would probably be a good idea to see a speech therapist and get rid of my accent.

No wonder people leave Milwaukee. There is no doubt in my mind that my difficulty getting a job is associated with this being the most segregated city in the United States. I won't pinpoint all of the racist mechanisms this kind of separation enables, but I know they affect every immigrant and person of color living here. The question I've heard the most in the last fourteen years is, "Why haven't you left yet?" Not only have I decided to stay, but I just accidently bought a house in one of the whitest parts of town.

Our neighborhood is historically blue collar, but has been attracting the college-educated crowd in recent years. We are close to the hip Bay View area, where property prices have soared. There are great restaurants and bars and probably too many coffee shops, and all kinds of shopping and entertainment, including the beautifully remodeled Avalon Theater, originally built in 1929.

The market for our price range was extremely competitive. Good properties got multiple offers in less than twenty-four hours. I checked listings constantly, day and night. When something interesting came up, I texted my realtor Joan and we were both there in less than twenty minutes. We visited staged homes with those little commands all over the place: "eat" in the kitchen, "sleep" in the bedroom, "brush" in the bathroom. I understand motivational sentences like "relax" and "love," but I don't need a sign reminding me to "drink" by the coffee maker (and definitely not by the bar).

I can't believe the hoops a person must jump through to get a house, even if they have most of the cash, as we did, after selling my old apartment in Brazil. Anything that was "move-in ready" had a ridiculous price tag. I am convinced that no matter what your budget is you are always about $20,000 below the place you think you deserve. We bid on homes we couldn't afford. I still have dreams about a cute blue Tudor that rejected us.

Here's another annoying trend: offer letters. That's a pitch the buyer writes to the seller of a house. You're supposed to tell them about the instant connection you felt to their home, how beautifully they have kept the place, how your kids would enjoy growing up with such a nice backyard. And, oh, you couldn't help but notice the pictures on the wall and you share their love of animals or travel or good food or community.

The letter should include the buyer's bio describing their (preferably) exciting profession: "Our careers as photojournalists have taken us around the world, but the time has come for us to settle down in our chosen home of Tuscaloosa." Add a picture or two for illustration.

I hated the idea of giving out private information. What if the owner was xenophobic? The whole thing is an exercise in nosiness—and, potentially, prejudice. I wrote the best letter I could stomach and even found a rare picture in which my husband Brock isn't wearing a baseball cap and you can't see my tattoos. We're pretending to toast wine, our cheeks touching, staring straight ahead with a tender expression that screams, "Please give us the honor of buying your house for ten thousand dollars over the asking price and we'll be your slaves forever."

Finally, after a few months of frustration and heartbreak, we found a mid-century ranch no one else wanted. The house smelled like cigarettes and mothballs and the kitchen was covered in a sticky layer of grease. It would take three months and at least $40,000 to make it habitable, but the price was about $60,000 less than the houses we were looking at. Nobody was willing to do the work, so I decided to realize my immigrant destiny and pick up the slack. After convincing Brock and enduring an emotionally draining closing process, the cost-effective but broken house was ours, and it was my job to turn it into a castle.

Remodeling our home has been one of my favorite art projects. The house is super solid; everything is made to last eons. The original owner was a lady named Alice who had a pink 1957 GE electric stove, which I restored and use everyday. I also keep my *Alice in Wonderland* books and trinkets in the kitchen in her honor. I decorated the living room with 1960s furniture inspired by the architecture of Brasilia, the modernistic capital of Brazil, a nod to the motherland. I'm no Mary Nohl, so I'm filling the walls with other people's artwork. I will spare you the rest of the decor details, but I love every corner of the place now. It is a working-class dream, color-coordinated and fine-tuned to our taste, retro-fitted to make us comfortable, and safe, and happy. From here I will be dragged to my grave.

A few years ago I was awarded the Mary L. Nohl Fund Fellowship. This is a grant for individual artists established with the millions of dollars Mary Nohl left to the Greater Milwaukee Foundation when she passed away. One of the main goals of the program is to keep artists in the Milwaukee area. It has worked for me and for most of the other Nohl fellows. I may not be able to make a living here, but I still have my art practice, as does Brock, who has been a prolific musician all his life. Plus, I could never afford a house like this anywhere else in the United States, making twenty-five cents to the dollar. It's a midwestern catch-22 and I'll take it.

Our Home in Havenwoods

TONI EDWARDS

A version of this story was first told live during a community event held in the Havenwoods neighborhood in conjunction with storytelling nonprofit Ex Fabula.

Before Toni told her story, UW-Milwaukee history professor Aims McGuinness provided a timeline for the Havenwoods neighborhood, from military installation into overgrown greenspace, then transformed again into predominantly African American suburbia with the city's only state forest. Today, McGuinness said about the far-north Milwaukee neighborhood: "People in this part of Milwaukee have figured out how to create communities and businesses and workplaces and parks that reach across boundaries of race, ethnicity, and class in ways other parts of the city and nation have not figured out."

One of the saddest days of my life: the day that I woke up, in Brentwood Court, in my brand new home.

The reason I was so sad was because I knew my marriage wasn't working.

I had spent my first night in that home with my husband and my four-year-old son. But I knew it wasn't working. We were going through the motions. We were doing everything you're supposed to do. We were married quite a while, we had a four-year-old son, and it was time to get a home so we could put him in his own room. Have a nice neighborhood to raise our son. But the one thing that I knew in my spirit was that my marriage was not working.

So it was time for us to buy a home. We looked for a home, we put in a bid, found a homeowner's concept magazine. And I said, "Let's look at one more home." We drove down Mill Road, turned on Forty-seventh, turned right on Brentwood Court. Perfect, tree-lined streets. And it was a dead-end street. Literally a dead-end street, because at the end of the block was Graceland Cemetery.

We went into the home. Three large bedrooms. Wood-burning fireplace. (A check on my list.) My husband, he wasn't quite sold. He liked the big backyard—and then he saw the potential of a man cave downstairs in the basement. We bought it.

Fast forward a year and a half later, I found myself in that home with just me and my son. I had some hard decisions to make. I had to decide:

Do I move back in with my mother? Or do I try to make this our home, me and my son?

So I worked first shift, second shift, swing shifts because I wasn't moving in with my mother, I wasn't that type of girl. Eventually, we did it. My family helped. Then, I decided, I had a friend going through a divorce herself—"Girl let me take you out. We're going to have some fun. I'm going to find somebody for you."

We went out to a club, over on the East Side—a place we call "Victims." (Some of you Milwaukee people may know.) We're at the club, talking, and a guy comes up and asks to sit down with us. We said, "Sure." Then she went on the dance floor and he turned to me and said, "How many children do you have?" I was so sad, embarrassed, mad, angry. How could I find myself in this situation? I would've never guessed I would have ended up here.

But then he said, "Don't be ashamed. I have a six-year-old son I'm raising myself." And I thought, "Hmmm . . . now he looks a little cute."

I gave him my phone number, we talked, we started dating. Then we decided that it was time to meet each others' sons. Because this relationship was about two families coming together.

He brought his son over to a barbecue at my house in Havenwoods. My family was there. I told my son: "There's a little boy coming over and he needs a friend." My son said, "Okay." When they got to the barbecue, my son walked over to him and said, "Hey, I heard you're looking for a friend." And that little boy said, "Sure." They took off, they ran and played in that big backyard.

Fast forward fifteen years: we've raised those boys as brothers in that house on Brentwood Court. They're both in their twenties now. Had you told me, sixteen years ago, when I woke up in that house on that first night and I was so sad, that I would still be there, I wouldn't have believed you. Believe it or not, I'm still there and I wouldn't have changed a thing.

Holton Street from Both Sides

JABRIL FARAJ

I watched from across the street, through my grandmother's screen door, as my family moved into a small brown-trimmed home on Booth Street more than twenty-five years ago. I was five years old.

As a child, Riverwest was an ideal place to be raised. It was diverse and accepting. I played with children of all colors, not caring for their social standing or economic class. We were free to roam the neighborhood. There was only one unspoken understanding: never cross Holton Street, though our home lay only one block to the east. Perhaps ironically, there are some who have whispered the same thinly-veiled warnings about Riverwest.

Much like Detroit's famous Eight Mile Road, which splits the wealthy, predominantly white northern suburbs and the largely black, poverty-stricken city, Holton Street cuts through Milwaukee's North Side. Separating the increasingly white and wealthy Riverwest from Harambee—where almost all of the residents are of color, unemployment is high, and housing values low—Holton stands as a distinct reminder of the attitudes at play here.

At fourteen, I began at Riverside University High School, a nearby public school. I learned, played, and fought beside individuals of all different backgrounds and ethnicities. It was there that I first read Charles Dickens's *A Tale of Two Cities*. The different worlds—the injustice and resulting violence—Dickens describes were familiar to me in a way I could not truly understand until I attended the prestigious Northwestern University, where most of my classmates had come from, and were going into, money.

I returned to Milwaukee after graduating in 2010 and, three years later, purchased a home in Harambee, eight blocks west of Holton. It was an intentional decision, born of my dedication to this city and an unwillingness to be influenced by the fear that so many allow to dictate their lives. My neighborhood is one that people with pale skin whisper about, telling other pale-skinned people to stay away. It isn't safe, they say. What they fail to see is the humanity.

We hear gunshots from time to time; we see and feel pain every day. There have been deaths on my block, but there is also life. I have sat with my neighbors, and them with me. We share yard work, conversation, and food. Our children play together.

As I walk from my home, near Fifth Street and Keefe Avenue, individuals and families sit on their porches enjoying a cool, early fall day. Two men stand on a corner drinking beer, while two others construct an entrance to the outreach center across the street. A young man requests some money for food. We make eye contact and exchange friendly greetings.

As I reach Holton, I see the newly paved street and wonder whether the people here now will be here much longer. As I enter Riverwest, I pass signs proclaiming welcoming and inclusion, yet find few people of color. My destination, a coffee shop on Humboldt Boulevard, is indicative of the change afoot. It was not here when I was at Riverside, which sits just across the bridge. I walked by this place often, and played across the street. When I was a teenager, there was nothing here. There was nothing until I was gone, and no longer in need of it.

But I came back. I came home.

I have often asked myself whether it is the space we inhabit that defines who we are, or we who define that space. What I have come to realize is that it is neither. I have found that, ultimately, it is the choices I make that define who I will be.

Moving to Milwaukee

MARIELLA GODINEZ MUNOZ

I only learned a few things about Milwaukee by the time my dad decided to move our entire family from El Salvador to Milwaukee in 1995.

Dad was already in Wisconsin, after many years in California, and he had already moved my brothers there in 1992. So my knowledge of Milwaukee was mostly from my dad's pictures and letters. In school, we had the opportunity learn about different important states in the United States like California, Texas, Illinois, Florida, and Arizona, but we didn't learn much about Wisconsin or Milwaukee.

My dad did a petition and requested US citizenship for me and my brothers and I traveled for the first time to the United States on January 24, 1995. The plane landed in Chicago at O'Hare, my dad picked me up, and we drove about two hours to the City of Milwaukee.

Soon after I left my family and friends, it was very difficult to adapt. My initial thoughts about Milwaukee were: I didn't know anybody, I was scared of living in a new city, I didn't know English at the time, and I was worried about not being able to make friends. Winter weather was new; El Salvador has tropical weather and it is mostly sunny every day.

It wasn't long until I made new friends and met many people from different heritages and backgrounds. But one thing many people had to learn about me: as a Latina Salvadorian living in Milwaukee, I've experienced situations when people have assumed I am Mexican. People asked, "How do you prepare the tacos or your dishes in Mexico?" Or, "Where in Mexico is El Salvador located?" I'm (still) happy to clarify in my response that I am Salvadorian and can share details about Salvadorian food, culture, and geography. I take it as a chance to explain to people my heritage, things like pupusa, a thick handmade corn flour or rice flour tortilla stuffed with cheese, chicharrón (cooked pork meat ground to a paste consistency), refried beans, or loroco (a vine flower bud native to Central America).

We have a Salvadoran community in Milwaukee and there are others spread out to Madison and Green Bay. There is a Salvadorian restaurant and pupusa food truck in Milwaukee. There are chances to explore and experience our culture. Nationwide, we're the the fourth-largest Hispanic population in the United States, according to the 2012 Census. Given the overall youth of the Salvadoran population, we may eclipse our Cuban counterparts for third place in the near future.

I'm not so alone as I first thought when we moved here. And, little by little, I have started to get to know Milwaukee and love my new home.

I can mention a few great things from my more than twenty years in Milwaukee. First, Milwaukee is a very diverse city; I have friends from all over the world. Milwaukee offers a variety of cultures and we celebrate almost everything. We have great festivals such as Puerto Rican Fest, Mexican Fiesta, Summerfest, Indian Fest, plus cultural festivals like Holiday Folk Fair where we can share our Salvadoran heritage.

Second, I've been able to share my communications skills with college students and on TV. As an instructor at Milwaukee Area Technical College and Alverno College—my alma maters—I'm proud of my responsibility to train and educate students from different heritages and different backgrounds so that they can graduate and become producers, directors, camera operators, film directors, and journalists. As a host for *Azteca Wisconsin* and the local magazine style TV show *Hoy Wisconsin Today*, based in Milwaukee, I have the opportunity to educate, showcase, and highlight stories from across our state. I love to bring to the community a bilingual local show that helps us to be more connected.

Third, I've had the opportunity to be a mom. I have two sons, ages eleven and nine. My kids were born at St. Mary's Hospital, where I had great nurses and doctors. Some of them are still very close friends. I am very happy that I live in a city where people care about each other no matter your heritage, background, or language. My kids are very happy to represent their heritage at school, being Americans but also sharing their Salvadorian (mom) and Bolivian (dad) cultures. We have participated in many school and community events, sharing with everyone our cultural traditions, music, dances, and food, especially introducing "las pupusas." When it comes to that ice in winter, our whole family now sees it as a reason to get out of the house, have some fun, and get some exercise.

I always have been a hardworking person, as a single mom of two children. I am always looking for the best for them. I always push myself the extra mile. I love to help others by volunteering in a variety of activities in the community, in the city, and on campus.

As a Latina, I love to be a role model to others and help them to be successful. Being a second language learner, a minority, and a woman who moved to the United States twenty-three years ago, I have suffered discrimination because of my skin color, my looks, and my accent. I have had a lot of up and downs in my life but I am still strong and I am able and capable to do more. I believe that by sharing my story, others will be successful. They'll also learn more about Milwaukee and Wisconsin. I am very happy with the opportunities that living in the city of Milwaukee have offered me. I love the city of Milwaukee and it will always be my home.

A Brief History of Milwaukee in Four Long Meals

TODD LAZARSKI

There's a curious, blurry distinction between HGTV-branded shabby chic and actual shabby. Between charmingly rough-hewn and rough, between the peeling paint of repurposed wood at your local mixologist's den, tinctured with appropriate weatheredness, and grandma's rusty crumbling house shed, where you warn familial little ones to steer clear out of fear of splinters and tetanus. There's fragile balance within the sort of crumbling palace charm evocative in places like New Orleans.

Of course, there was never anything palatial about sleepy, suburban St. Francis, Wisconsin. Or Polonez. Or Polonez's first location back on South Sixth Street in the early eighties. Or any of the other Polish outposts about Milwaukee. Or really any of the other midwestern Polish enclave towns—Cleveland, Detroit—all littered with last names ending in '-ski,' lousy with kielbasa breath, of which, population wise, Milwaukee ranks as the fifth-most Polish-est.

Rather, here on the blue-collar South Side, the worn out structure sits, quietly, as if it has maybe given up, to time and to the chasing of it, to style or posture, abutted by the city limits to the north, the gray ripples of Lake Michigan to the east, beleaguered and blighty residential-ness in the immediate vicinity. The Polonez's Clinton-era website touts options for a "funeral luncheon." And that should tell you enough. It's flyover territory, literally, as General Mitchell International Airport sits just a few miles to the southwest.

It feels ripe for Bourdain acolyte one-upsmanship, a Google map on some taco tour of realness, a dance of identity performance ending in an ejaculation of "You've got to try this place." Dilapidation is the mother of charm, after all. But is there any fashionability in a boiled pork shank? In a potato pancake?

But you can still taste, for now anyway, the old country, and a different caloric life, at the last Polish restaurant in town: bloody borscht, bacon barley, bigos—a potent meat and sauerkraut mash—hunks of bitter fried Polish cheese meant to be greedily dunked into Russian dressing, mushroom and onion filled deviled eggs of the softness fit for someone who forgot their teeth, veal cutlets covered in fried egg and melted cheese and a lingering soupçon of gluttonous shame, parentheses-shaped polish sausages. The pierogies shine brightest, literally, simmering and sheeny as they are from a quick bath in hot grease. The old school hot pockets yield meaty teams—a pork and beef combo, a turkey and cranberry concoction. Or, even better, an inspired homogenized puree of a reuben sandwich—like you just had oral surgery but you also have a delicious pastrami sandwich in the fridge and an efficient blender handy. It's all engagement eating. Not because of the nature of the restaurant as much as the almost stinky character of dining. This is a bad-breath meal of reward, of eggy, unapologetic heaviness, somehow both a fortification against a long cold night, and a bringer of chilly, digestif meat sweats. It's the kind of side-hurting, fat-fortified fare inherent in Milwaukee's cholesterol.

It's also, from the ceiling tiles and chandeliers on down, a place you'd take Grandma, a place rife with other people's grandmas on a Saturday night when a guy gently wails on an accordion over a drumbeat and some sing-along on his way back from the buffet line. Even though most grandmas probably think they can cook as well, Grandma will go. And sometimes that is the ultimate compliment. Although she's never considered realness, or being into the place because of the hidden gem factor fit for the blogosphere, with an authenticity meter, or braggable hole-in-the-wall Instagram optics. Grandma, if she was doing it right, has always been too consumed by the marriage of fat and protein, the nurturing spatter of fry grease. She eats here because before we had to make everything complicated, to frame a hunk o' sweaty meat just right for social media consumption, to write wordy tomes of Monday morning analysis on a "crushed" meal, there were pierogies and sometimes, polka. And life was hard, short.

You maybe won't get exactly a grandmotherly vibe or welcome at Tsunami. You may very well get busy waitress attitude, a bit of eyebrow arch even, like they're not exactly used to patrons with my own Irish complexion and broke-ass Spanish that I'm too intimidated to actually use. It's about fifteen blocks west of where those of my '-ski'-last-name-ending-kind get tacos, in a town where people actually, unfortunately, frustratingly, stick to their kind.

Yes, by most metrics, Milwaukee is the most segregated city in the country. And here, or at any of the dozen taquerias in flattoppeded-chorizo-waft distance of Tsunami, it's easy to feel. Especially when you're the lone gabacho pounding a lime Jarritos and barely using chips to slurp relentless salsas, itching to remember to use the phrase "los dos" when she asks what kind of tortillas I want with my camarones al diablo (thinking it'll impress the server enough to disclose the salsa recipe . . . no, the other salsa recipe . . . no, the other, other one).

After the two table salsas—a soft, salty sizzle on an onion-laced red, and a citrusy, chunky ceviche blend—two squirt bottles signify it's time for tie-loosening business, for bathing and basting buds in a flurry of capsaicin combo punches. The red jabs aggressive, thick and salty and blankety on any chopped meat. But it's the verde where things turn ethereal: cool, creamy, addictively vicious, it's an emulsified cream sauce, a velvety, oil-blended concoction of the likes that can be found in many other taquerias about town. It's both a perfect chillout and spice up, for the aforementioned chorizo, the steam frizzle of which will still be wafting about your head upon table delivery, seeing as how said flattop is arm's lengths away, a serious-looking man with a spatula regulating his little monopoly of smoke. Or douse any of the meats that are housed in double corn tortillas—the lightly fried fish, the smoky, charcoal-reeking carbon, somehow-not-dry pollo, a deep stewed, earthy beef known as desebrada. It's the rare place where you don't have to sample the specialty in the spot's name—mariscos—to eat the best of what they have to offer, to, as the best meals can do, be brought somewhere else, to another tribe, another somehow unseen pocket of a city. Though if you do, anything swimming in the mean-spirited, fire-engine-red diablo sauce—meant to be tolerated as much as enjoyed, like love—is a real passport-puncher.

For a brief period of a nineteen-year-old stoned haze, I told people I was interested in joining the Peace Corps. As an adult, this is the sentiment I leave with my wife as I head west again, "breaking boundaries one tortilla at a time," I say, near every Saturday she seems to think, though to me it's not often enough. And I practically award myself a Medal of Honor as I stumble out, gaseous, bloated, toting salsa to-go containers, a torta for late night munchies. Heading back east, toward the lake, on Lincoln Avenue, skirting urban decay and potholed concrete, for what may appropriately be called the aisle of denial—the Riverwest neighborhood in the north, past the fashionable East Side, through downtown, the yuppied Third Ward, Walker's Point, down to hip Bay View, portions where the 17 percent

Latino population is barely noticeable—I think, for the brunch-going sect, the in-for-Summerfest crowd, maybe there aren't enough seats in Tsunami anyhow. But like that unknown meat moniker, buried deep on a voluminous Mexican menu, how can you know if you don't try?

The segregation script gets flipped upon an entrance to Tandem. A few miles from the 2016 Sherman Park riots over the fatal police shooting of Sylville Smith, in a town where police protocol for a black man double parked is tackle and tase, regardless if said black man is a rookie on the local NBA team. At Tandem you walk in and are immediately treated as if they are grateful to have you as a guest, to be able to serve someone, practice on. It's a bit ironic once you taste the food, feel the skin crackle of the fried chicken behind the teeth, hear the oily snap, see the steam billow off the shimmering pale meat stuff, whiff the cayenne pique, poke some salty breading crumble from the corner of lips back into the mouth. It's a product that would clearly sell itself.

Though, almost like saying grace, it's requisite to wait for food discussion, to hold off on gorging, given the deep sense of purpose here, which borders on an altruism, one deep enough to threaten overshadowing any kind of kitchen work. In short: Chef Caitlin Cullen left her post at uppity, whole-hog emporium Bavette to do something new in the oft-overlooked and majority African American neighborhood of Lindsay Heights. She asked what type of dishes the community would like to see on the menu of her new venture. She decided to focus on hiring exclusively from within that neighborhood. She sought to go further, banking on her Detroit-area teaching background to offer extensive kitchen training to new employees, even those with no experience, hoping her spot is a kind of launching pad for restaurant roles across the entire city. "Pipeline employees." It's a noble community endeavor, with legit chef pedigree. In the era of "locally-sourced food," here is a move toward locally-sourced people. It's as if your favorite local musician knocked on your door, offering to take requests, for your very own house concert.

But we're also not into dinner at Goodwill. And when you're nestled on a hot summer night amidst an old brick-walled, Edison-bulbed courtyard, sating happy hour hunger with something cold in tin cups, with icy Two Hearted Ale, dunking smoked kielbasa wedges and blackened onions into spicy mustard, this feels much more like a grease-trekked venture of epicurism, one that seems to have no relation, in fact, to have never even heard of any such do-gooderism. With Prince or D'Angelo bumping low, with deviled eggs so creamy, mustard-y, or fried chicken livers so snappy, it tastes like a fully realized, foodist repurposing of the old neighborhood tavern. And apparently neither "foodist" nor "repurposed" have to be such annoying terms.

Rather, consider the true gem of the dinner menu, a Memphis-style fried chicken. With potent, sneaking heat, an amber hue not overbearing like the more popular chicken of its Tennessee city brethren, it's spice that is deep, but one that lets chicken be chicken, not a fire drill for taste buds, a macho showoff pissing contest of tolerance. Still, what makes the dish so noteworthy here is the absurd crispiness. Fried within an inch of destruction, the delicate clinging connection between so much snap and crackle and such tender underbelly seems to act as metaphor. For togetherness, for a renewed sense of community. It lends a feeling of hope, and a night that can taste good enough to maybe heal wounds, while pleasantly shredding intestinal regularity.

Irony only gets so much mileage. So when you find yourself belly up at the bar of Vanguard, watching an O. J. Simpson workout video, awaiting placement of an order for a draft craft cocktail, noting the mural on the wall of wrestlers The Bruiser and South Milwaukee's own The Crusher, it's important to remember that no, the owners here actually like wrestling. And maybe, by the time the, say, duck BLT sausage, or the Velveeta-draped sausage patty burger, or simply a chili cheese hot dog with decidedly un-simple housemade whiz, begin to assert their steamy selves in front of you, it doesn't matter anyways.

On a recent step out in Buffalo, New York, another blue-collar burg, rife with hard-drinking, big-eating, cholesterol-disregarding Polish heritage, I was left scratching my head over whether or not a "Portlandia"-esque eye roll was due for Ru's Pierogis, a decidedly new school bar and eatery there with the likes of a chicken wing pierogi. Is it irony? Is it hipster romanticizing of a proletariat past? Is it genuine repurposing of a perfect food love package—like all that wood in all those small plate spots? Or, wait, actually, does sociological cataloguing matter?

The tongue scoffs at such concerns. There or here at Vanguard. Especially when it gets a smacky bite of the aforementioned burger, dripping with a spicy sauce and rich fat, or a Jamaican lamb currywurst, or a Nashville hot chicken—in fried sausage form. After all, you're bellied up to the bar, and it's frigid, Lake Michigan air trucking like it grew endlessly kicking legs on the couple block flight over, like a sparring partner from a boxing class never signed up for, no matter which direction you look. It's the same when it's sweaty, and outdoor beers are hard to keep cold, and you're on your way home from Summerfest, the biggest music festival in the world, and you want another, with sausage to wash it down, or vice versa. It's the kind of place you take out-of-towners, because the food is good, but also to prove something about our town. That we are not a European holdover—strictly schnitzel, an approaching-Fargo accent, curd-centric cuisine, jovial bellies, big box beer purveyors. The kind of city ripe for punch lines. Like on *Cheers* when Norm asks Cliff, "Quick, what does my breath smell like?" to which the half-inebriated mailman replies: "Milwaukee." Or like when former NBA-er and current talking head Jalen Rose listed Milwaukee as a stop where league players had to "import" their entertainment. When you're at Vanguard, with *Sticky Fingers*-era Stones blasting, the muted TVs moved onto an episode of *Soul Train*, the tiny corner flattop sizzling into infinity, and you're sipping the day's special whiskey and a Pale Ale from Three Floyds, polishing yes, fried curds with beer stein aioli, for whatever it's worth, it feels like we can be cool. With fist-shaking defiance of the past and the tropes, Milwaukee can be fun.

Last Call for Milwaukee's South Side Taverns

EDGAR MENDEZ

Originally published at Milwaukee Neighborhood News Service.

In the late 1970s and 1980s business was so good at Orchard Inn, a neighborhood pub on South Third Street and West Orchard, pool leagues ran morning, evening, and midnight to accommodate three shifts of blue-collar workers who strolled in from nearby factories, including Allen Bradley—now Rockwell Automation and Grede Foundries—since closed, recalled its former owner Sharon Ward.

When Ward, SafeRide coordinator and treasurer of the Milwaukee County Tavern League, and her late husband purchased Orchard Inn in 1975, it was one of thousands of neighborhood pubs in Milwaukee, she said. Like many others it served a vital function for patrons looking to catch more than just a buzz.

"The corner bar was the area's social hub; it's where you felt the pulse of the neighborhood and found out what was going on in your community," Ward said.

Parents knew each other's kids and kept a watchful eye, holidays were celebrated together there, and when a family was having a tough time financially, they turned to their friends at the bar for help, she added. But in the city that once touted itself as the "beer capital of the world," and is still home to MillerCoors, the tavern culture generations of Milwaukeeans grew up with is fading away in some neighborhoods, as an older, simpler style of life moves to the slow lane to accommodate the accelerated pace of today's society.

Nowhere is that change more evident than Milwaukee's South Side, where day care centers, houses of worship, corner stores, and residences occupy properties that for decades had been bars. A drive down South Thirteenth Street or West Cleveland Avenue serves as a reminder of just how prevalent corner bars were at one time, and provides evidence that many old-time bars are now closed. Faded marquees and other signage are all that is left.

According to a 2017 *Milwaukee Neighborhood News Service* analysis of data provided by the City of Milwaukee, 40 percent of businesses with tavern licenses in 2012 in the 53204 ZIP code (which includes the Walker's Point, Walker Square, and Clarke Square neighborhoods), where Orchard Inn was located, and the neighboring 53215 ZIP code have now closed for any number of reasons. In 53215 (which includes the Polonia, Lincoln Village, and Silver City neighborhoods), forty of eighty-five taverns, including stalwarts such as Ducky's, Grady's Saloon, Kornerstone Pub, and Frank and Barb's Silver City Bar, have closed in the past five years.

"Back in the day you could walk to a bar on every corner and it'd be busy. Didn't matter if it was eight in the morning or eight at night," recalled Brian Schmidt, as he sipped from an eight-ounce tapper of Pabst at Richies Pub, 1998 South Eleventh Street.

Richies is one of a dwindling number of South Side bars that have been open for decades, said its owner and namesake, Richie Dobs. He said he's stayed in the bar business by keeping his prices low and hiring good bartenders, though he plans to retire soon and hopes to find a new owner for the bar, which typically closes by 7:00 p.m. and serves a racially-mixed clientele that includes blue-collar workers and retirees.

Jim Rydzewski, owner of Bob-E-Lanes, 2932 South Thirteenth Street, bought his tavern/bowling alley from his parents in 1981. He said he's seen many a bar in the neighborhood close during the three and half decades he's been in business.

Rydzewski is in his sixties now, and said he hopes to find a new owner when he's ready to retire in a few years.

"It would be a shame for this place to close after all the money I spent improving it," he said of the bar, which runs daytime pool leagues daily and in the morning every other Monday.

Not everyone views a decline in the number of bars on the South Side as a negative. Alderman Jose Perez, who represents the 53204 ZIP code, said one of his memories growing up in the Walker Square neighborhood was seeing a dead body lying in the street outside of a tavern on South Tenth Street and West Walker. Perez said his mother collected signatures in the neighborhood to have the bar shut down.

"Bad things happen at bars and they have for a long time," Perez said.

In addition to increased crime, which has made some neighborhood pubs less desirable to visit or run a business in, the corner bar in Milwaukee is becoming a relic for a number of reasons, according to James Draeger, historic preservation officer for the Wisconsin Historical Society and author of the book, *Bottoms Up: A Toast to Wisconsin's Historic Bars and Breweries.* The long list includes issues related to licensing, tougher drunk driving laws sparked by the Mothers Against Drunk Driving movement, and, ironically, an increase in driving, which opened up the city for residents to visit bars in other areas, whereas in the past they likely would've walked down the block.

"A lack of transportation in the early nineteenth century created a legacy of walkable neighborhood taverns in Milwaukee," Draeger said. In addition, he said, tenements and small houses in nineteenth-century Milwaukee limited the ability for people to host friends, which made the tavern a more suitable place to get together.

There are other basic reasons for the decreased number of bars that are associated with modern times, such as more entertainment options and the fact that mass communication has made taverns less critical to social life, Draeger added.

"Taverns aren't really about the drinking; they exist because of the social life of the tavern. People want to meet people, or meet with friends, and those functions were as relevant today as they were fifty years ago, but people do it in many different ways now," Draeger said.

The industrial crash that began in the seventies and continues today devastated many local communities and the taverns that served them.

"We lost tool and die makers, mechanics, laborers, and machinists. When we lost a big chunk of the labor pool we lost a bunch of customers as well," said Ward, who tended bar at The Last Drop on South Fifteenth Street and West Rogers until it too closed a few months ago.

Ward and her husband purchased the bar in 1985 and ran it as Wardski's until she sold it in 2009. She stayed on as a day-shift bartender until it closed, serving the aging client base she'd built for decades consisting almost entirely of retirees.

A decline in customers and profits made running a neighborhood tavern less attractive to the next generation, she said, so when tavern owners died or were too old to run their pub, their kids didn't want it.

"The next generation didn't see the value in owning this type of business nor putting in the time and effort it takes because it's a twenty-four-hour job. They went to college instead," Ward said.

Rydzewski said his kids helped out at the bar when they were younger, but they wouldn't be taking over the family business either. "They all got kids and are married. They got good jobs. They're not interested in running this place," he said.

Despite the decline in neighborhood pubs on the South Side, the number of businesses with a tavern license in the city increased from 1,096 in 2001 to 1,356 in 2016, according to data provided by the city. Those numbers could be inflated. The *Milwaukee Neighborhood News Service* found many are actually closed. Much of the new business can be attributed to an increase in the number of specialty bars such as Drink Wisconsinbly Pub and Grub, Oscar's Pub and Grill, Buffalo Wild Wings, and other locations that generate business from food, craft cocktails, and a large selection of tap and bottled beers, Draeger said.

One example of a traditional-turned-specialty bar is the popular Walker's Point pub, Steny's Tavern and Grill, 800 South Second Street. Jerry Steny opened the bar in 1985 and said that at the time Walker's Point was the top bar area in Milwaukee. Eventually though, his younger clientele shifted to Water Street downtown and Brady Street on the East Side when crime increased in the 1990s and 2000s. The bar struggled until his son Ryan Steny came aboard in 2010 with the idea to specialize in craft beer and sports. Business has been booming since.

"It's important to set yourself apart from the rest. Competition is fierce and you need to stand out," Steny said.

Those who didn't innovate and were resistant to change, including many older tavern owners, haven't survived as a result, Draeger said.

"Many of the neighborhood tavern providers are elderly and aging out and don't want to change. They don't want to have twenty-somethings and thirty-somethings in their bar; they want people like them," he added.

The newer bars that are chains, leased or run by general managers and others who don't live in the neighborhood are a far cry from the days when bars hosted block watch meetings and Christmas dinners, Ward said. The evolution of bars such as Steny's and the influx of chains has dealt a heavy blow to the neighborhood pub, one from which it's unlikely to recover, Ward said.

"Those days are gone. Running a bar in the neighborhood was a good way of life and a good thing for the neighborhood. But our bars are dying off and we're dying with them," Ward said.

Milwaukee Bus Ride

JAN CHRONISTER

Church steeples puncture the membrane
of the stretched-out winter sky.
Old man in gray pants
creaks down for a penny
in front of a nativity.
St. Mary's rosebushes
wrapped up in sackcloth
like hooded friars.
On a balcony rail
smiling pumpkin decays.
Fingers on the bus-seat upholstery
read the jolts like Braille.

On the Redlining Bus Tour in Milwaukee

LAUREN SIEBEN

A version of this article previously appeared in Belt Magazine.

On a Saturday morning in early February, with six inches of snow covering the ground and temperatures hovering around twenty degrees, a group of twenty-five adults in puffer jackets piles into a yellow school bus for a tour of Milwaukee.

Instead of buzzing through breweries or stopping to admire Cream City architecture, the driver follows a route through Milwaukee's once-redlined neighborhoods—the parts of the city that banks and insurance companies refused to serve on the basis of race until the Fair Housing Act of 1968 outlawed the practice.

Before hopping on the bus, our group meets in the conference room of Town Bank in the Walker's Point neighborhood. Adam Carr, one of our two tour guides, connects his laptop to a screen and begins clicking through a brief presentation. One slide displays the Wikipedia definition of redlining: "the practice of denying services, either directly or through selectively raising prices, to residents of certain areas based on the racial or ethnic composition of those areas." Several slides show black-and-white photos of Milwaukee's historically black neighborhoods from the 1930s, 1940s, and 1950s, depicting bustling main streets and thriving storefronts.

Joaquin Altoro, Carr's co-guide for this specific tour and a vice president of commercial banking at Town Bank, shares a quick disclaimer (the opinions expressed on the tour don't reflect the opinions of his employer), before pointing to his shirt, which says, "Milwaukee?"

"I love that shirt," Carr says from behind his laptop. "For me as a Milwaukeean who loves Milwaukee, that is the shirt that best represents how I feel about it. I feel a lot of 'Milwaukee exclamation mark,' but I also feel a lot of 'Milwaukee ellipses,' a lot of 'Milwaukee, goddamn,' you know?"

Carr then shares a paraphrased version of the James Baldwin quote: "I love America more than any other country in this world, and, exactly for this reason, I insist on the right to criticize her perpetually."

The redlining bus tour is part of a series Carr calls Milwaukee Tours for Milwaukeeans, which endeavors to give Milwaukeeans a deeper understanding of their city. A lifelong Milwaukeean himself, Carr got the idea during a stint producing radio segments about Milwaukee neighborhoods.

"I had this explosion in my understanding of the city and how incredibly different and similar it could be across lines," says Carr, of his time working for independent local radio station 88Nine. "I was fleshing out the humanity of places that I had only understood as being defined as their deficits."

But while Carr spent most of his time in the field with people from across the city, he worried that his work might make some listeners complacent.

"Ideally, a story would compel someone to cultivate their curiosity and see something for themselves," Carr says. "But I was worried I was reinforcing people across divisions by making them feel content in their understanding of a place they haven't been to."

Carr is not the only local using interactive tours as a means for educating Milwaukeeans about their city.

Reggie Jackson is head griot of America's Black Holocaust Museum, a recently re-established Milwaukee museum founded in the late eighties by James Cameron, who was the only known survivor of lynching in the United States. Jackson offers "segregation tours" that focus on the intersection between segregation and the loss of Milwaukee's manufacturing jobs starting in the 1960s, which led to many of the abandoned, boarded-up factories and homes still sitting vacant today.

"There are parts of the city that people never go to. They hear about them on the news, but they don't really hear why those neighborhoods became what they became," Jackson says. "The assumption in many cases is that black people didn't take care of their properties, but people tend not to make the connection to the huge loss of manufacturing jobs."

Jackson considers himself a "public historian"—by helping locals better understand history, he hopes they gain a deeper understanding of modern segregation that isn't rooted in stereotypes. The risk, says Jackson, if you're not careful about offering historical context, is that these types of tours devolve into poverty tourism.

"I read something years ago about 'ghetto tours' where they'd invite whites, generally, to go to so-called dangerous parts of the city to show what it looked like but with no historical context," says Jackson. "It was like when people see a car accident, they slow down to look to see if there's a body on the ground."

Back on the redlining bus tour, we drive along Walnut Street through the Bronzeville Business District for an "after" view of the black-and-white "before" photos we saw at the start in the bank conference room. Carr points to vacant lots and apartment buildings where black-owned businesses and clubs once stood. We make a stop in the parking lot of Columbia Savings and Loan, the first African American-owned savings and loan association in the city, founded by Ardie and Wilber Halyard to help black residents secure loans at the height of redlining. (A nearby neighborhood is now known as Halyard Park.)

For many aspiring black homeowners in mid-century Milwaukee, Columbia Savings and Loan was the only place to turn to, as other banks adhered to "residential security maps" designed by the FHA-back Home Owners' Loan Corporation (HOLC) in the 1930s.

HOLC created these maps with the help of local mortgage lenders and real estate appraisers. The maps used color coding to rank neighborhoods based on risk and credit worthiness: green ("best"), blue ("still desirable"), yellow ("definitely declining") and red ("hazardous").

In Milwaukee, as in other cities across the nation, black and immigrant neighborhoods consistently received the worst ratings. Paired with "racially restrictive covenants" that barred black residents from buying property in the suburbs, redlining intensified segregation throughout the United States and made it nearly impossible for African Americans to obtain mortgages, thereby stunting their ability to attain and grow wealth.

In addition to color coding, each neighborhood map came with a qualitative summary. District Five is one of the most egregious examples among Milwaukee's 1937 security maps. The neighborhood was described as a "negro and slum area" inhabited by "laborers and ne'er-do-wells."

Under the District Five map's clarifying remarks, the assessor added: "Besides the colored people, a large number of lower type Jews are moving into the section."

Our next stop is a few blocks west where we meet Ariam Kesete, a young black developer who is converting a dilapidated building in the Washington Park neighborhood into a start-up incubator. We file into the vacant building, which is currently stripped down to its studs and undergoing repairs for water damage. The space will house accounting, marketing, and health care services for small business owners, along with a coffee shop.

For Carr, getting off the bus is an important part of the experience. "I wanted to get people out of that spectator role of just seeing things through the windshield," Carr says.

Kesete tells the group she wants the incubator to nurture entrepreneurs from the neighborhood. "We're creating a hub for people to have a startup business so they can grow and then relocate elsewhere as the neighborhood gets up to speed," she says. By supporting the residents of Washington Park, Kesete hopes to mitigate any risk of gentrification, which could displace the immigrant families who live in the neighborhood today.

Altoro says the key to avoiding gentrification is supporting developments that are "favorable to the culture and the race of the people" already living in the neighborhood. He cites Chicago's Pilsen neighborhood, a Mexican enclave, as an example of a thriving local economy. He starts naming local businesses, art museums, and dulcerías as evidence.

"Who knows what a dulcería is?" Altoro asks the group. A few of us raise our hands. "If you don't know, it doesn't matter. It's not for you, it's for them!"

The tour wraps up back south in Walker's Point, a historically Hispanic neighborhood that is often described today as "up-and-coming." It's home to some of the city's most expensive restaurants, cocktail bars, and loft apartments.

Altoro was born and raised on the South Side. His grandfather was one of the first Mexicans to arrive in Milwaukee in 1915 to work at the Pfister and Vogel leather tannery. His grandfather also had seventeen children in Milwaukee—Altoro credits him with the early growth of the Mexican community here. "If I were to run for office I would have an amazing built-in constituency," he jokes.

The bus pulls up to the block where Altoro's grandfather lived when he first arrived in Milwaukee. Altoro holds up a blown-up poster of the redlining map description for District Eleven, where our group now stands.

In 1937, District Eleven received the lowest ("hazardous") rating from HOLC, along with comments about the area's Polish population and one final remark that's personal for Altoro: "Mexicans are encroaching in the northeast."

"The wording just blew me away," says Altoro. "That right there is a direct reference to my family."

The tour doesn't conclude with a neatly delivered summary or a call to action for the group, which is mostly white and ranges in age from millennials to baby boomers.

"Adam and I are really okay with not having this specific outcome, like we want people to organize and do something," says Altoro. "We're really comfortable with the fact that we left it here, now let's see what type of impact and effect it has."

What matters to Altoro is that on this tour, he had the opportunity to tell Milwaukee's story of redlining in his own words, alongside Carr, who is biracial.

"For Adam and I, we are not the normal person that's been telling the story," Altoro says, explaining that he usually hears about segregation and discrimination in Milwaukee from the perspective of a white reporter. (This point is not lost on me, a white reporter.) "I'm proud that this story is different than the one I'm used to being told."

Altoro says he's also proud to support minority business owners through his work: "There aren't that many bankers who look like me working in commercial business banking in Milwaukee."

Jackson says that on his tours, placing segregation in historical context is just as important as bringing people outside of their usual "bubbles."

"It gives us the ability to have more normal interactions, where you just deal with people based on your shared humanity and you don't look at people from this perspective of a stereotype," Jackson says.

For Carr, he hopes the people who attend his tours leave with a heightened understanding for how the city's past directly shaped its present. He hopes people pause to consider the complexity of Milwaukee's history the next time they read a headline.

"Milwaukee is a place where there's a lot of understanding at a distance," Carr says. "That goes for people no matter where you are, no matter what side of the line you reside on."

Tarzan and the Great River

CHERYL NENN

On August 19, 1922, Johnny Weissmueller, a former Olympian made famous for his role as Tarzan, tried and failed to break the record for the 150-yard backstroke during a swim in the Milwaukee River just upstream of North Avenue in the former impoundment formed by the North Avenue Dam. The swim was covered by the *Milwaukee Sentinel* and the *Chicago Tribune*—it was a big deal.

Nearly 100 years later, on Saturday, August 11, 2018, another swim race was held on the Milwaukee River—the inaugural Cream City Classic Open Water Swim—with more than seventy people participating in a one-and-a-half mile swim in the Milwaukee River near its confluence with Lake Michigan. The river advocacy nonprofit I work for helped to organize the swim and, as far as we know, it was the first public swim race since the time of Tarzan. Prior to the swim, a reporter asked me: "When did the Milwaukee River actually become 'unswimmable?'" That question is not easy to answer.

Milwaukee's rivers have always been important cultural, economic, and natural pathways. Native Americans used these water routes for trade and transportation, and sustained themselves with the fish, wildlife, wild rice, and other plants harvested from the rivers and associated wetlands.

Traders, trappers, missionaries, and French explorers used the rivers for exploration and trade. As European settlers moved into the Milwaukee area, the local rivers quickly became the main commercial and shipping arteries of the young community, and were heavily used for transporting wheat, lumber, coal, and other products. Over time, roads, railways, and air transport gradually replaced rivers as the major transportation routes for most goods. Milwaukee and other cities gradually turned their backs on the rivers, which had become severely polluted. Buildings that had once opened out to the river now looked to the streets.

Over recent decades, people are once again embracing their rivers. This change in perception is the result of improved water quality, a surge in building and redevelopment along riverfronts, increased interest in recreation, and improved public access. The rivers are now used largely for recreation—from the more natural reaches upstream to the more urban portions of our rivers welcoming boaters to dock along the RiverWalk to enjoy a local beer. Even fifteen years ago, it would have been unthinkable to organize a swim event on the Milwaukee River. Even five years ago, many were afraid to even kayak in our local rivers, fearing the impacts or the growth of a third limb, should someone flip. Today, we have five different vendors renting kayaks, canoes, and paddleboards to hundreds of paddlers flocking to Milwaukee's rivers during summer weekends.

Overall, water quality has improved dramatically due to improvements in wastewater treatment, construction of the Deep Tunnel storage system for sewage and stormwater in greater Milwaukee that reduced raw sewage discharges, and the removal of more than a dozen major dams that historically blocked water flow and caused localized water quality problems. The impoundment that Tarzan swam in—the North Avenue Dam was removed in 1997—was probably pretty bad in water quality back then due to industrial pollution, untreated sewage, and stagnation. Nearly a hundred years later and despite significant efforts by many, the Milwaukee River and its tributaries are still not considered clean enough for swimming in vast portions of its reaches. Even though we hosted our first swim in nearly a century, it does not mean that people should swim wherever and whenever they want. For this swim, a site and time was chosen to minimize but not completely eliminate risk.

The goal of the swim was to raise awareness of the amazing resource that we have in our own backyards as well as to inspire stewardship and activism of our rivers and waters. We have a right to clean water. And although we have come a long way toward improving water quality, we still have a long way to go until we get to a point where we don't have to worry whether it's safe to swim or safe to eat the fish we catch from the Milwaukee River.

When we talk about our right to clean, fishable and swimmable water, this language comes from the 1972 Clean Water Act (amended in 1977 and 1987). While President Richard Nixon is widely given props for signing the Clean Water Act into law, the issue was forced by Congress, who voted to override his veto. Congress was reacting to increasing demands for environmental protection due to dirty air and water, to the creation of the first Earth Day by Wisconsin's own Gaylord Nelson, and to events like the Cuyahoga River catching fire in Cleveland in 1969.

As an aside, less well known was an incident in October 1951, where Lincoln Creek caught fire after a 60,000-gallon fuel oil spill was ignited by a local homeowner burning trash near the creek. The creek fire caused a five-alarm blaze that damaged several homes. The main concern at the time for Milwaukee's Mayor Frank Zeidler (who became famous as the United States' longest serving Socialist mayor) was to get the oil from Lincoln Creek on the city's North Side down to the river it fed into, the Milwaukee River, and then past several dams where the fire boat could use its nozzles to push the floating slick toward the Lake Michigan harbor. The solution to all pollution back then was dilution. And prior to the Clean Water Act, not many Americans were thinking of what it even meant to have a "swimmable" or "fishable" river until they no longer had one.

The Clean Water Act provides the foundation for protecting the chemical, physical, and biological integrity of our nation's waters. It set a goal to attain a level of water quality that "provides for the protection and propagation of fish, shellfish, and wildlife, and provides for recreation in and on the water" by 1983—this is known as the fishable and swimmable provision—and to eliminate the discharge of pollutants into navigable waters by 1985. Sadly, we are long past this time, but we are still not meeting these fishable and swimmable goals, and probably weren't meeting them long before the Act was enacted in 1972.

Scientifically though, there is still is a good deal of controversy over what the definition of "swimmable" is, and that depends on what criteria are being used. Despite decades of science and rule-making, the nation's recreational criteria designating a "safe" level of bacteria—or at least a level of bacteria that minimizes sickness after a day at the beach—are pretty lackluster and enforcement of this criteria is weak at best.

Practically speaking, a river likely becomes unswimmable when people stop actually swimming in it. Clearly, most Milwaukeeans had no idea in 1922 or 1951 if the Milwaukee River or other rivers were swimmable. Local government wasn't testing for *E. coli* bacteria back then, if anything. They did know how the river made them feel, how it smelled, how good the fishing was, whether one would walk from one side to the other atop trash. We do know that the Milwaukee River had a series of swimming schools along it from the North Avenue Dam to present day Estabrook Park. The swimming school constructed in 1914 in what is now Gordon Park ended operations in the late 1930s. There are wonderful pictures showing children tethered to ropes and swinging into the river from the shore. The school was very popular due to the river having a much warmer water temperature than Lake Michigan beaches over a good part of the summer. Remnants of this swimming school still exist just south of Locust Street on the west bank of the Milwaukee River. Several amusement parks existed in what is present day Hubbard Park in Shorewood, including a slide that went into the river.

So why did swimming stop? The most likely answer is the severe contamination caused by untreated sewage, agricultural runoff, and other contaminants. One could make an argument that the river became unswimmable in the late 1930s, though it is very possible that conditions were not good for many years before those swimming schools officially closed. Today, when many people develop stomach or gastrointestinal problems, they rarely associate those problems with a day at the beach or a day paddling the river. Tying illness to water quality continues to be challenging even for the experts.

Regardless of what water quality tells us, there have likely been swimmers in our river all along and so maybe it never became unswimmable in a literal sense. Even after Tarzan swam in it. Even after Lincoln Creek caught fire. Even after the slow death of the swimming schools. Even before the Clean Water Act.

There have always been hearty souls swimming in the Milwaukee River from downtown to the headwaters. The Cream City Classic was designed to create a splash by showing our public officials that there are people who want to swim in our rivers for recreation and it is their right. Right now our rivers are not all safe for swimming in many locations and times of the year. But we can get there by demanding infrastructure and water quality improvements and by working together as a community toward a future where swimming in the Milwaukee River and its tributaries is safe.

Where love is love is love

ALEX ROSE

Here I walk.
The boldness of the art museum,
Next to the ghostly shell of the
Summerfest grounds
Where soon drunken nights will be had.
This skyline so different from the one I grew up with—
It is the one that has become home.

She is there.
In this park that was always beautiful
But now for different reasons.
The sun begins to set now and
Silhouettes of those around us begin to dance along the path.
They are all here, friends and lovers.
I am in the company of both.

I am queer.
This is my confession.
It was here, now, that I tell her.
This city,
The one that brought me to her
And us to certainty,
Was the first to know.

Where we go.
Together we walk along the water,
I am shaken.
In this moment I am a stranger to myself.
Love is love is love
But who am I really to know.
She grabs for my hand,
I pull away for now.
I watch as the birds chase each other

And imagine myself joining them,
If only for a little while.

Together we share.
This time that has passed.
This city,
The birthplace of our family yet to come,
Sets the scene for you and I.
Drive over the bridge,
While I nod graciously to our first of many spots.
Buildings grow smaller in the distance

As we make our way towards the house
We made into a home.

Dare to be.
Together and proudly,
Two people in one city
That speaks up when called on.
Where love is love is love
And we are here to own it.
Home to a community that thrives
And stands together,
When times are good,
When times are bad.

Here we walk.
In this city that we call home,
With the stories that we have etched
Into this ever expanding landscape.
Her by my side,
Here with me,
It's all I can see.
The paths we have walked
Again and again
Leading us to wherever it is we may go.

"Together We Rise": on Painting a Sherman Park Community Mural

TIA RICHARDSON

"It felt heavy, and while we were helping it didn't feel as big. It's deeper than what I thought it was." -Gabri-El Taylor Bey, Sherman Park resident and mural participant

This is what I heard after I sat down with residents to watch a short film documenting their experience working with me on a community mural called "Sherman Park Rising." After working on the film with co-producer Andy Gralton and putting the pieces together, watching it with neighborhood residents revealed a larger story than the individual ones they each brought to the mural.

"I didn't realize I was part of something bigger." -Charmane Perry, Safe and Sound youth organizer

Little did I know when the project started in June 2016 that it would have such an impact. When I was called in by former Safe and Sound community organizer, Amanda Schick, it was still one month before the police shooting of Sylville Smith that would come to a tragic end, sparking violent unrest and capturing media attention in Milwaukee's Sherman Park neighborhood.

Amanda and other organizers had been working with residents for eighteen months to identify top priority issues, like beautification, speeding cars, and gun violence. A strong network of community groups with deep roots in addressing neighborhood issues wanted a mural for so long, to beautify a blighted, problem corner of Forty-seventh and Center Streets.

But after the community was shaken in August 2016 and left to grapple with the aftermath of violence and negative stigma, I had to rethink my approach as the mural's lead artist. Given the hot climate confronting issues of police accountability, coupled with feelings of hopelessness and depression affecting this neighborhood and others due to structural inequity, compounded by a traumatic event . . . this couldn't be just another mural with some decorative images. I knew there were opposing feelings and points of view about what had happened, even among people working on the same sides. How could I get people to work together if they felt differently about the same painful issues?

The feelings were still raw nine months later when funding was approved by the City of Milwaukee and I was given the green light to start gathering input from the community.

On an otherwise ordinary day in a church basement for our first public workshop, a surprising dilemma confronted me. I knew there would be a range of emotions about different problems, from hot anger to cool optimism. How to avoid a downward spiral of frustration if they didn't agree? Would I focus on the problems, or would I focus on the positives?

Up to that point I was afraid people would show little interest in painting a mural, let alone about anything positive after what they went through. Yet young and old, black and white, community organizers and business owners, all shared a spectrum of issues they cared about. They shared the joy and the pain with mutual respect. Later I realized an uncomfortable truth: that I had underestimated the community's willingness to acknowledge painful issues in a positive way.

"It was just so powerful with the climate as it is . . . and it just shows that one by one we can make a difference, and through something like art, through involvement in a community art project . . . art can be therapeutic without being art therapy." -Devvie Washington Walton, Sherman Park resident and mural participant

I approached this project from the angle of a process of healing, guided by my background using arts as a way to relieve emotional stress from trauma. The steps to get there: first, offering a chance for people to acknowledge the problems they care about. Once we can acknowledge how we feel, we can make a choice about how we want to move forward. Here, it meant thinking of a tangible, practical thing they or others are doing or wish they could do in their neighborhood to improve the situation. Then, together, we get to imagine where our combined actions lead us in a vision of the future.

"It provokes a hope of change . . . but when you look at the bigger picture it's something positive to reflect on . . . The painting and the video is one positive thing that's different from the narrative." -Vaun Mayes, Sherman Park resident and mural participant

The mural shows the little-known, resident-driven assets—urban gardens, grassroots youth programs, nonprofit and individual support for housing and literacy, and working with police to improve accountability and community relations.

The narrative surrounding Sherman Park persisted as a negative one.

But many residents wanted a way to tell others outside of that area what they weren't seeing, through the mural.

Negative stressors can create a negative self-image. How we feel about ourselves influences how we treat others and our motivation to move forward. I feel that the negative stressors in our environment today far outweigh the positive reinforcements it takes to turn around the effects of internalized trauma. I believed there needed to be something positive to counter the effects of that influence.

This is why I asked participants something from a positive viewpoint: "What does hope look like?" We have to imagine tangible pictures in our vision of the future, or else it's just another hard-to-grasp idea that will fly away in a cloud of forgotten dust as soon as negative reality swoops back in.

The beautiful thing about sharing what matters to us in a room full of strangers is that it opened up space to be a little more vulnerable. In that vulnerability, we saw the chance to reshape the narratives we hold close. Taking that risk opened our hearts and minds to new ideas, new feelings, new perspectives—a new vision!

"I never thought of art as being hope, and I think of hope as an action word by getting everyone involved." -Kenneth Ginlack, Sr., Sherman Park resident and clinical therapist

One of the most powerful moments during the project was when people got involved to help paint the mural.

On scheduled days the mural was open to the public to pick up a brush and "paint by numbers." By the third week more than 150 people painted the first layer of color over the entire wall. There were toddlers, teenagers, families, elected officials (Mayor Barrett and Alderman Russell Stamper lent their hands), law enforcement, the business improvement district. The community groups who were so instrumental in seeding the idea of a mural in this location showed their support. The joy in the air was contagious.

"Peace is a process of each person doing what they can do." -Doris Wallace, Sherman Park resident and mural participant

When the mural was complete something surprising happened that called me to do one more thing. At the mural ribbon-cutting, everyone who had been involved from the beginning was there in support. Mayor Tom Barrett spoke at the request of the city, and everyone else had a turn to speak, including myself. Someone I did not expect to see, because he had not been involved up to that point, was Milwaukee's former police chief Ed Flynn. I didn't expect Flynn to give his sincere appreciation for what he saw as hope and community spirit in the project.

But in the moment I doubted his sincerity.

Despite my doubt, I wanted to know what he really felt, so I reached out for an interview. This stretched far beyond the limits of my comfort zone. That interview proved pivotal for me as a person of color, sitting across from a white male former police chief. It revealed as much about my own bias as much as a bigger theme of how to find common ground that opens up a chance to learn about each other's humanity.

"I mean if we can create peace in really small ways because we see somebody like Police Chief Ed Flynn in a different light because he's touched by the art in the same way I'm touched by the art . . . that moment is a really big one for moving our whole city to a different place of respect and understanding between people who come from different places." -Shelly Roder, Sherman Park resident

Panning across the seventeen-foot by fifty-six-foot mural, you see images of struggle, of loss, and of hope. We see a woman lifting a house off an elderly man who's being helped by a young boy. We see babies and toddlers playing in flowers, youth working to free a lending library from hungry vines. We see trust, respect, and working together. We see young people desperately calling out to adults for help, a memorial tree with balloons and a silhouette of one life too many lost. We see the call and the response of the community, different demographics, bringing peace lilies to support the rebirthing of the community. Homeowners and renters, young and old, black and white, Jewish and Christian, professional and non-professional.

In the middle, a policewoman, a male resident, and a builder share the burden in lifting a household full of people on their shoulders. Their dance is a symbol of the balance of power between authority, residents, and the creative energy it takes to move everyone forward, with hope.

In all of the symbolic messages everyone can find something they can relate to in their own way. We can't go back and change the past, but we can honor it for what it can teach us about our humanity, and then use this moment to choose where we want to go next—together.

One Man's Treasure: The Milwaukee Museum Built from Scraps

RACHEL SEIS

"Introducing . . . HEROIN." The framed advertisement blared from a wall in a replica pharmacy storefront. "For non-addictive relief from the coughs, since 1898."

I gasped, laughed, and snapped a quick picture of the relic as I peered at the painstakingly preserved antiques surrounding me in the room. Moments later, as I made my way into the next exhibit, I'd hear another visitor approach the sign with the same reaction.

The antique advertisement hangs above an impressive assemblage of tonics, medicinal elixirs, bars of soap, boxes of toothbrushes, and curious curitaves from the Prohibition Era. They're meticulously displayed in a small room designed to resemble Milwaukee's Bay View Drug Store circa 1920—just one intriguely intricate space in the 1869-built Italianate home that's been converted into a museum amassed from one man's lifetime of collecting.

Avrum "Abe" Chudnow was the son of a scrap peddler, and became fascinated with finding, foraging, and filing away everyday artifacts at an early age, and continued collecting objects from the twenties, thirties, and forties—the era he spent growing up in Milwaukee—into adulthood. Chudnow graduated from Marquette University law school and went on to practice law from his office at 839 North Eleventh Street. As his collection grew and began to fill any extra space in the basement of his Fox Point home, he moved his precious pieces to his office, where he dreamed of opening a museum to show them off to the public someday.

Chudnow passed away in 2005, but his family vowed to make his dream a reality. In 2012, with the help of an executive director and a curator, The Chudnow Museum of Yesteryear was opened to the public—from the same building he practiced law decades before.

The museum sits on an unassuming stretch of Eleventh Street between Kilbourn Avenue and Wells Street, just a quarter-mile west of the comparatively massive Milwaukee Public Museum—which houses a pretty impressive frozen-in-time exhibit of its own. Perched above the bustling Interstate 43 that bisects the city's east and west neighborhoods, the museum's neighbors are as eclectic as the relics found inside. Just a block to the west, you'll find students traipsing across the private-college campus of Marquette University. Directly northwest lies the bustling Aurora Sinai Medical Center. And just north of the museum, you'll find King Park, one of the most impoverished neighborhoods in Milwaukee. It's a curious location for a collection of one man's treasures of the past, but inside, there's a celebration of landmarks across the city as they were nearly one hundred years ago.

From the moment I turned the corner at the museum's entrance, in fall 2018, I was whisked into an era removed by nearly one hundred years. I'm a sucker for these walk-through dioramas of immersive history, but there's something especially charming about this one. Typically, I'm separated from these historical relics by thick glass and velvet ropes—plus hordes of bored teenagers, rambunctious kids, and spatially-unaware adults—plodding along in my way. Here, as I made my way through the museum's meandering layout, the old wooden floorboards creaking beneath my feet, there was little between me and a massive collection of everyday objects from generations past.

There was the ice cream pavilion replica from Shorewood's doomed Wonderland Amusement Park, including a sign that welcomed me to purchase a bottle of Green River soda or an ice cream sundae from the resident soda jerk, an invitation to enjoy either as I moved from room to room.

Then there was a stop in the hardware store, showcased with an antique Stewart gas stove at its center. Its display cases were filled with electric household gadgets like "pants pressers" and new inventions like the toaster oven, and if I needed to touch up that paint job in the family room, I was relieved I could turn to the can of definitely-not-poisonous Dutch Boy lead paint displayed proudly on the shelves.

The largest exhibit in the museum is the H. Grafman Grocery Store, whose original location was just a few blocks away on Vliet Street. It's got a large stock shelf at the center, lined with packages of baking soda, salt, popcorn, pretzels, and other dry goods—many of which have labels that I still recognize on shelves today (the can of Heinz peanut butter, though, did throw me for a loop). Tucked in the corner of the grocery store is an old crank-style telephone in working order. Pick up the receiver, give the crank a whirl, and it will ring in the museum's front hallway. If you're lucky, museum curator Joel Willems will pick up on the other line.

Willems is an affable, enthusiastic employee who's been at the museum since its grand opening, and he worked with Chudnow to catalog his collection before his death. As I guided myself through the museum, he would pop in an exhibit, take notice of an artifact I was eyeing, and share a little history behind it. Standing in the train depot exhibit, we chatted about Milwaukee's impending streetcar system and how old is new again. When I made my way into the World War I room, he shared how many of America's German immigrants changed their names to reflect a more English-style spelling. After sharing how I had studied the history of baseball in college, he invited me to come back for an upcoming lecture on the 1957 Milwaukee Braves. Although I preferred guiding myself through the museum at my leisure, I was happy for the moments Willems took between manning the ticket counter to make sure my visit was even richer.

As quaint as the museum may be, it's impressive just how much is packed into every room. Upstairs, in Dr. Joseph J. Eisenberg's clinic (Dr. Eisenberg actually lived and practiced in the home before it was purchased by Chudnow), there are details like a pile of his actual business cards sitting on his desk, genuine X-rays, and—an ironic addition in a room meant to represent the place where he healed the ill—his death certificate framed on the wall. The Grand Avenue toy store features a case that illuminates many of Chudnow's personal childhood playthings, including a classic Monopoly board game, Lincoln Logs, and the lesser-known Lincoln Bricks set. There's even a sized-down replica of Saxe Theater with rows of theater seating, where I rested a spell to take in a rotating loop of short films on subjects from the life of Avrum Chudnow to footage of the World Series-clinching game between the 1957 Milwaukee Braves and the New York Yankees.

From the twenties-era telephone switchboard to the old RCA phonographs to the barber shop boasting Depression Era prices for a shave and a haircut, it's awe-inspiring to be reminded that every single thing your eye falls on is part of one man's collection. And by "part," what's on display is only 5 percent of his entire collection—and that includes the paraphernalia hidden away in the secret speakeasy, which I was delighted to sneak into near the end of my tour. There are thousands more antiquities that are waiting to be swapped in for a seasonal exhibit or, potentially, an expansion of this endearing museum that paints a portrait of Milwaukee that—if not for one man's dedication to preserving the past—could all but be forgotten.

The New Brews That Make Milwaukee Famous

HENRY SCHWARTZ

I was having a beer with three local "beer barons": Mike Brenner (Brenner Brewing), Mat McCulloch (D14 Brew Pub), and Nick Reistad (Raised Grain). We got to talking about how nice it was that we could all be in the same industry creating similar products and still want to share a beer together. We talked about the beer scene in Milwaukee, the lack of "local love" at the time, and the difficulties of opening and operating a brewery.

As we saw it, minus Miller still being here, the beers that made Milwaukee famous have nothing to do with Milwaukee anymore. If Milwaukee wants to continue to be known for beer, it can't rely just on the history of beer, though that is an awesome part of it. Milwaukee has to appreciate the three pillars of beer awesomeness that exists and thrive here today:

1. Historical beer, from old buildings to the beer barons' graves . . . there is a ton of beer history in our city.
2. The craft pioneers, Sprecher and Lakefront, that kicked it off in the eighties when there was no such thing as craft.
3. The new wave of brewers that are pushing the boundaries of this fine malty beverage.

So, back to our meeting of the new wave of beer barons . . . instead of sitting there complaining—or just having another—we decided to do something about it. This eventually led to us formalizing a group, becoming a regional subchapter of the Wisconsin Brewers Guild, all the starting point for the regular meetings, events, and collaborations we've done today.

From there, we fanned out what it means to do beer business in Milwaukee—beyond craft brews and connecting all involved in the world of beer, like bars, distributors, and enjoyers—which is where "Drink Brew City" started. Our goal is to be collaborative, not oppressive. We want to work with distributors and bars because we're all needed to get people the beverages they want. At the end of the day, it's possible for everyone to succeed. But, if anyone in the system gets greedy, it doesn't work. We definitely live in a lopsided system where backdoor political discussions and tons of money dictate the laws governing Wisconsin alcohol production and sales. Small breweries can't compete in a system that runs like that. We've already seen a few breweries and beer ideas quickly come and go.

Ultimately, I hope we're part of an effort where more bars support local breweries and value the hard work their neighbors put into creating products. I hope laws change so that beer sales are less of a "pay-to-play" game. I hope more neighborhood breweries open up and have successful businesses. Just like movements in many consumable industries, knowing where your products come from is important, because the dollars you spend on local products stay in the community. And I hope growth in beer continues to be a driving factor in the economic growth of Milwaukee and Wisconsin in general.

2018 Drink Brew City member roll call:
    Bavarian Bierhaus
    Broken Bat Brewing Company
    Company Brewing
    District 14 Brewery and Pub
    Eagle Park Brewing Company
    Enlightened Brewing Company
    Gathering Place Brewing Company
    Good City Brewing
    Inventors Brewpub
    Lakefront Brewery
    MKE Brewing
    MobCraft Beer
    Museum of Beer and Brewing at Old World Wisconsin
    Raised Grain Brewing Company
    Sprecher Brewing Company
    St. Francis Brewery
    The Explorium Brewpub
    The Fermentorium
    Third Space Brewing
    Vennture Brewing Company
    New Barons Brewing Co-op

Opening Day and Back Again

MATT WILD

In the shadow of Miller Park stands another Miller Park, and it is on fire.

Whispers of this second Miller Park have been heard for hours. Have you seen it? You've gotta see it. It's over in the Don Money Lot, I think. Upon arrival you find an army of serious, lawn-chair-seated men huddled around the burning stadium. They poke and they prod and they stoke the flames. Crowds gather and gawp. Someone asks if they can take a picture. "Fifteen bucks," smirks one of the lawn-chair-seated men.

The second Miller Park is a grill, of course, and it smokes in the late-morning Milwaukee sun. It is homemade. It stands waist-high, is spray painted green, and is the spitting image of its real-life counterpart—right down to the fan-shaped retractable roof/lid. In the place of "Lo-Mo" Kentucky bluegrass, charcoal. In the place of players and managers, brats and burgers. In the place of the Famous Racing Sausages brought to you by Johnsonville, non-racing sausages brought to you by Klement's.

Nearby, people scream as a beer bong explodes. Someone topples into a giant Jenga game to the strains of "Whoomp! (There It Is)." Beanbags are tossed into the sky—so many beanbags. The lawn-chair-seated men grunt and turn their attention back to the grill. Amidst all the mayhem, a child tugs at her father's sleeve. "Daddy, can I get a picture with the giant sausages?"

Someone pukes. It is Opening Day.

***

To focus solely on the drunken shenanigans of Opening Day at Miller Park is to miss the point. Yes, there are many drunken shenanigans to focus on: binge drinking, binge eating, ill-advised twerking, overflowing Porta-Potties, still with the beer pong. But in order to truly appreciate this annual springtime spectacle, in order to truly understand its unique flavor and vibe on this Monday afternoon in early April, one must zoom out and marvel at the sheer enormity of it all. The word "tailgating" calls to mind a party. Tailgating at Miller Park on Opening Day is a bender.

The price for that pernicious party is pavement. The stadium's parking lot covers more than 3.2 million square feet of not-quite-downtown Milwaukee land and boasts more than 12,000 parking stalls. It is divvied into sixteen sections, many of them named after former players and personnel. There's the front-and-center Henry Aaron Lot, the nearby Rollie Fingers Lot, the far-flung Robin Yount and Paul Molitor Lots. There's the distant Bob Uecker Lot, which, like the obstructed-view, in-stadium section named after the legendary Brewers broadcaster, is proudly dumpy and self-deprecating. "I must be in the front row!" Uecker crowed in a series of 1980s Miller Lite ads. A walk from the Uecker Lot to the main gate takes innings.

Indeed, traversing the whole of Miller Park's parking lot can feel like a six-month trip through Middle Earth. Bridges, woods, ravaged wastelands, and even a river (the Menomonee) mark its landscape. Various kingdoms and despotic outposts can be spotted and explored. Various tribes and colonies can be joined and made war with. It's a bewildering continent of buses, bar shuttles, pickup trucks, party tents, rock and country music radio trailers, news crews, grills, coolers, lawn chairs, makeshift bars, makeshift sound systems, and those ladderball games where you tie two golf balls to a piece of rope. To gaze out at the parking lot from the upper levels of the stadium itself—when you finally get there—is to gaze out at hundreds of flag-marked encampments separated by seas of asphalt. Fellow travelers move through those seas like wraiths, 1982 replica jerseys on their backs and bottles of Leinenkugel's Summer Shandy in their fists. Smoke fills the air.

⌂⌂⌂

"Any day above ground is a good one. Thank you for your service."

The mood in the Jim Gantner Lot is belligerent at best—a co-ed fistfight has only recently cooled down—but even the most wasted reveler pays respects to the military vets making their way to the nearby Sausage Haus. People pause, nod solemnly, and cough. If there's one thing that can stop a party cold, it's national pride.

There's another strain of pride at work here: tailgating pride. The Gantner Lot is the park's smallest—a mere 49,950 square feet and 139 stalls—but its ambitions are enough to fill the Yount and Molitor Lots ten times over. It's absolutely loaded with people, and its shish-kebab-choked rows and aisles have formed a crude sharing economy; no man, woman, or fan still wearing a J. J. Hardy jersey is wanting for ketchup, mustard, or a Pretzilla soft pretzel bun. "This is the place to be!" screams a woman over the din of 69 Boyz's "Tootsee Roll." She takes a bite of a burger and cackles wildly.

Over in the Cecil Cooper Lot, news crews have descended on those who have descended on a massive Johnsonville trailer and its complimentary wares. Free stuff is everywhere on Opening Day, whether it's branded T-shirts, branded can koozies, or branded food. The news crew interviews a delighted brat-eater as he stands in a massive line that snakes its way around the trailer and halfway down the main concourse. "What do you think of Johnsonville replacing Klement's as the official sausage of the Milwaukee Brewers?" asks a reporter. "Whatever!" says the man.

The ostensible reason for this entire ruckus is a three-hour baseball game featuring Your Milwaukee Brewers, but the colonists who have claimed the tucked-away "Stormin'" Gorman Thomas Lot ensure that there are plenty of other distractions. Classic parking lot games are joined by rowdy karaoke face-offs (Toby Keith's ever-execrable "Red Solo Cup"), tedious rounds of *Rock Band* and Cards Against Humanity (the former complete with drums), and oodles of unnecessary drinking games. A homemade Brewers arcade game stands in the middle of it all, its cabinet decorated with copyright-infringing logos and its screen bordered with baseball cards of old players (Aaron, Yount, Geoff Jenkins, Rob Deer). A man fiddles with it. It's out of order.

Meanwhile, over in the wild-and-wooly Uecker Lot, another man walks past a clutch of relish-stained pavilions and sits down on the wooded shore of the Menomonee. He peers out at the chilly waters as if contemplating a new world—or maybe an old one. Behind him, a parking lot filled with thousands of his closest friends and party pals; in front of him, the looming visage of Miller Park. The first pitch of the game is imminent. The man studies the topography between him and the stadium: hills, valleys, that saxophone dude who seems to be at every game and who only seems to play "The Pink Panther Theme." Somewhere—everywhere—a plaintive "WOOOOO!" echoes through the air. Also, "The Pink Panther Theme." The man gets up and starts to walk.

In the shadow of Miller Park stands another baseball park, Helfaer Field. It's a small-ish field that hosts Little League games and charity events, private parties, and kickball tournaments. Helfaer is sold as a real-life "Field of Dreams" and can be rented for two hours at a time. It is built on the site of Miller Park's predecessor, Milwaukee County Stadium.

County Stadium hosted its final major league baseball game on September 28, 2000. After that game, Bob Uecker took to the pitcher's mound and gave a speech. "It is a very sad time for me," Uecker said as the stadium lights were turned off. "For I have been here as a fan, as a player, and for the last thirty years, as a broadcaster. But tonight is the final curtain. It's time to say goodbye. We will never forget you. For what was, will always be. So long, old friend. And goodnight, everybody." County Stadium was demolished five months later.

Like County Stadium itself, ghosts of Opening Days past still hang around the site. Memories of the year your buddy passed out on a lawn chair and never made it inside. Wisps of the time Mom tipped the Porta-Potty and couldn't stop laughing. Half-remembered afternoons filled with pressurized beer bongs and Jell-O shots and eating and drinking and grilling and dancing and screaming. This is where the Brewers once played, and now don't. This is where everything was once so right, and where everything started to go wrong. This is the same lot we parked in last year.

Someone puked. It was Opening Day.

On These Acres

SUE BLAUSTEIN

I walk down Holton Street Sunday
      as the sun goes down early,
tender with color in the gravity of mid-November.
Advance Die Casting's overhead doors
and recessed exits are silent. From one,
      an illuminated doorbell watches
      the western sky with me—
its wheat-colored beam as sentimental
as the rural late autumn of calendars—
      a cabin, and whitetail bucks
with hooves in a light crust of snow.
The half-timbered tavern on Richards Street
      is sentimental too. Once thousands
of autoworkers parked across the street.

      Every eight hours, on these acres,
hundreds of ignition keys were turned, wrists
      and wrists revolving clockwise
together. The tavern windows are crowded
with pimpled aloe plants and cactus;
      and one has a faded cutout
of Arnold Schwarzenegger. It's decades old,
      from *Commando* or *Terminator*, shows
we saw at Northtown; the Budget, or Mill Road,
      which are gone. Everyone loved
hearing Arnold say hasta la vista. We laughed
      because he was oblivious—unblinking
as cycles or laws—when he was sent
      by the losers of the future
      to go back and revise the past.

Milwaukee Day

BRENT GOHDE

The goal among Milwaukee Day's three founders was that the new holiday could take on a life of its own—a self-defining, organic celebration of community and positivity. And as I write this in 2018, it certainly belongs to everyone. It's "Milwaukee Day" to most, "414 Day" to many. It doesn't take a genius to grasp the concept—or to have come up with it in the first place. And while nobody in the area code is about to decline a random excuse to party, it's worth considering what value a holiday-from-scratch based on civic pride could add.

The primary reason the holiday enjoyed solid footing and wide adoption from the outset is, most Milwaukeeans are from Milwaukee. That sounds obvious, but it's not the case in other towns. Portland Day? Portland is a destination city. Same with Chicago and Austin, Boston and Miami. Seattle, San Francisco, down to Los Angeles; east to New York City, Washington, D.C., Philly—even those cities with a predominantly native population might have multiple area codes, the impetus for the little holiday a few of us started in the late 2000s. It's the Goldilocks adage paraphrased—not too big, not too small. Just in that sweet spot where a made-up holiday can take off.

There's not a ton of mystery or mythology surrounding Milwaukee Day, its origin or otherwise. The short version is, local musician and medical professional Andy Silverman's brother Toby texted him on April 14, 2009, saying something along the lines of, "Hey, it's 4/14. It should be Milwaukee Day."

The reason for this won't be lost on many readers. The area code for Milwaukee County is 414, April 14 is 4/14—Toby is a genius, clearly. Regardless, he lives in Florida. So upon getting the text, Andy recruited a buddy from the local hardcore scene, Justin Thomas Kay, to design a quick logo. They secured the dot com, built out a Tumblr with the logo—and nothing else. Now, it was official. But officially what?

Andy called noted man of action Timm Gable. Timm called me, since I'd pulled off events in partnership with the Milwaukee Art Museum and worked at WMSE, a celebrated local radio station. And together we decided to, um, have a parade rolling down Wisconsin Avenue. Turns out a parade is an undertaking best handled by organizers with a lot of time and a lot of money, and we had neither. But Timm produces films and Andy had a suit. So in April 2010 we made a silly video with a couple potted plants flanking Andy at a podium in an inconspicuous corner of the UW-Milwaukee Union, in keeping with our under-the-radar campaign.

Turns out—shocker—Milwaukee was ready to embrace another reason to put on a festival. The area code is not shy in this regard, embracing Bay View's Mitten Fest with nearly as much zeal as Summerfest. "Frozen Snot Ride? Hey, I didn't get my flu shot to just sit around on the couch." Our Milwaukee Day video landed on the local news, and it was a hit before we even planned anything.

With that encouragement, we made more of a formal big deal out of the next Milwaukee Day, with a few public events and even landing a mayoral proclamation. For something that basically started as an inside joke, this set the bar pretty high. From then on we had to outdo ourselves to keep it interesting for anyone paying attention. Park cleanups, ringing the bell in City Hall's tower, throwing out the first pitch at a Brewers game, a Turner Hall show with rising hip hop star WebsterX—the day grew annually, and we kept losing money out of our own pockets. Which was fine. There are more expensive hobbies we could have taken up. Plus, it was becoming a platform to collaborate with new and different people from all over the city.

To think at any length about why it's worked is to realize something special about our hometown—our particular shared history. The person you encounter at work or one barstool over can name a family member touched by the *Cryptosporidium* outbreak, know where they were when Dale Sveum hit that walk-off homer to win the Brewers' twelfth straight in 1987, had the same geometry teacher in high school. You likely have a very strong opinion as to where Speed Queen ranks in the best-ribs-in-town debate. You have a Domes story and or a Sidney Hi story, an Oriental Drugs T-shirt and or an Atomic Records T-shirt. You have old clothes in Goldman's bag downstairs, or you've been to Conejito's in the past six months.

And as sure as everyone knows a guy who knows Port Washington native Dustin Diamond, the irony is, everyone also knows ours is the most segregated city in the country. In that latter fact, the daydreams of nostalgia come crashing into reality. The list of what we have in common is long, as divided as our city can be along race and class lines.

This mix of somewhat insular, shared history and distinct city divisions is what made the next phase of Milwaukee Day something special.

Our costs aside, the idea of Milwaukee Day was free. Then, a few years ago, venues, bars and businesses were doing their own Milwaukee Day things. Mainstream broadcast outlets started to earnestly celebrate; 88Nine Radio Milwaukee launched an all-Milwaukee artist radio station on 4/14. In ensuing years we'd approach rooms to throw events, only to learn they already had their own thing going on six months in advance.

This is good, right? Grasping for that goal of a real, citywide day run by many people toward something fun and positive? For a made-up holiday, in a city not shy to celebrate, this wider, inclusive party is a dream we couldn't have fully known when it started via a goofy text in 2009. So, while we'll continue to coordinate, along with a small team of organizers that now includes Chelsie Layman and Rachel Fell, we will also look to do more to enrich others' lives more than we did at the outset. Of course, we're still stoked about the silly, outstanding things, like when Milwaukee Day appeared as a clue on the 2018 Valentine's Day episode of *Jeopardy!* And there's nothing wrong with getting together with good people to partake in what made Milwaukee famous (cover bands, in case that wasn't clear). But it can also be twenty-four hours where we do something to make things tangibly better for everyone.

Being a Goldilocks burg is a terrific opportunity—Milwaukee is big enough where there's always work to do, but small enough that we can accomplish a lot. And with any luck we'll all be doing some good in an annual spotlight. My dad, born and raised in 'Stallis and now spending retirement leading tours of Miller Park, has always assured me: people want to help if you let them. Let's give people something to get behind with their own time and resources and make the city's narrative more appealing. There's a platitude I tagged in press releases in the early goings of the event, a decade ago now, one that meant nothing at the time—"Live every day like it's Milwaukee Day." In our own small but important ways, we've started to see what that can mean, for a day, in Milwaukee. Let's partner up and dig in so "Milwaukee Day" is shorthand for an ethos we can all be proud of.

Ghosts of Bay View

KEN GERMANSON

Howard Zinn had a shameful confession to make in Bay View in the late 1990s.

Zinn, author *of A People's History of the United States* and one of the most informed historians on US working-class history, was in our Milwaukee neighborhood to join an annual commemoration of Wisconsin's largest labor massacre. At that year's event, Zinn said it was the first time he had really heard about those who organized—and died—in the 1886 Bay View Rolling Mills tragedy.

It's a good bet, then, that the bloody events and even the standing state historical marker have been lost over the years on many of the customers at the nearby popular restaurants and pubs in this increasingly hip neighborhood, to say nothing of the thousands of people who drive past daily on to work, into downtown.

As obscure as the meaning of the site might be for some, on the first Sunday of May for the past thirty-two years, it becomes a lively and important historical reminder for several hundred unionists, neighborhood residents, history buffs, activists, and just plain curious citizens. The event has grown from historical commemoration to one that features a re-enactment with twelve-foot tall puppets and volunteer actors wearing the gray outfits of nineteenth-century workers, followed up with stirring speeches and inspirational singing.

In 2018—the 132nd Anniversary Commemoration of the Bay View Tragedy—some 300 crowded onto the cramped site, mostly standing, greeting each other like the long friends and colleagues they are, but often realizing the last time they saw each other was likely at this same event a year earlier. Shortly before the program begins, a group of several dozen march up—many wearing the pink hardhats of the "Women of Steel," a Steelworkers union group—having completed a short march that roughly follows the events of May 5, 1886.

This annual ceremony is held to pay homage to seven who gave their lives in the historic quest to establish the eight-hour workday. The Bay View neighborhood event, sponsored by the Wisconsin Labor History Society, serves as a reminder of those who died, shot down by the state militia while in a march of some 1,500 workers on May 5, 1886, toward the giant Bay

View Rolling Mills plant on the shore of Lake Michigan, in what would become Wisconsin's bloodiest labor incident.

"While we want to remember their deaths, we need to celebrate their courage," said John Schneider, prominent Milwaukee actor and director, who narrated a reenactment of the 1886 incident. "Their deaths were not in vain. They won; the movement won."

Within ten months of the massacre, the workers' People's Party took over the Milwaukee City Council. Many of those who marched in 1886 went on to create the Socialist Party that by the early 1900s teamed up with "Fighting Bob" La Follette and his Progressive Republicans to make Wisconsin a forerunner in pro-worker and good government legislation. Socialist leadership in the city led to making Milwaukee one of the nation's most egalitarian of cities, as well as one of the best-run cities, a claim made in a 1935 *Time Magazine* cover story about Socialist Mayor Dan Hoan.

It can seem like distant history, at times. In 2011, Republican Governor Scott Walker infamously stripped a majority of the state's public sector unions of collective bargaining power, under protests that shut down the state capitol. And, 132 years since the Bay View massacre, the eight-hour work day is still an issue, Milwaukee Area Labor Council President Pam Fendt reminded the audience.

"How many of us work more than forty hours a week and still bring work home?" she asked, singling out teachers and nurses. (It wasn't until 1938 that the Federal Wage and House law was passed that created the forty-hour workweek, though never explicitly an eight-hour day.)

Fendt quoted a *New York Times* article that said many are working sixty hours a week; she cited the galling pay disparity between CEOs and the average worker. Fendt urged the labor movement to redouble efforts to bring change, particularly through organizing.

"I see hope out there," she said. "I see leaders who want to make Milwaukee again a great union town."

Picking up the organizing theme, Kristin Fecteau, an apprentice electrician and member of IBEW Local 494, said every member must be an organizer, taking every chance to engage coworkers, friends, neighbors, and others in discussions about unions. This is an important way in which to combat negative beliefs about unions, she said. Unionists can't be complacent, she said, calling attention to a union election that was lost by a few votes because many members failed to show up to cast ballots.

Her comments ended on a stirring plea: "Be proud. Be committed. Be productive and be union!"

This year's program was emceed by Anita Zeidler, a UW-Milwaukee retiree and a member of the American Federation of Teachers whose role in many past commemorations involved laying a memorial wreath at the foot of the state historical mark at the site of the event. Her late father, Frank, was Socialist mayor of Milwaukee from 1948 to 1960. (Frank Zeidler was part of the event's planning committee and a regular event speaker from its founding in 1986 to his death in 2006.)

Barbara Leigh, former director of the Milwaukee Public Theatre, joined in direction by Schneider, produced the dramatic reenactment of the march and the shooting, a staple since 2011. Popular Milwaukee drummer Jahmes Finlayson provided accompaniment while Craig Siemsen, retired Milwaukee Public Schools teacher and union member, led the crowd in traditional sing-a-longs of "Ghosts of Bay View" and "Solidarity Forever." (The late Milwaukee folksinger Larry Penn composed "Ghosts of Bay View" and it has been sung at every event since 1986.)

History tells us repeatedly that oppressed people need to come together in solidarity to seek positive change. Whether it was in the winter of 1936-37 when autoworkers in Flint, Michigan, sat down on the job, setting off successful union organizing in the factories across America; or in 1955 when Rosa Parks refused to sit in the rear of the bus in Montgomery, Alabama, igniting the Civil Rights movement that was to bring momentous legislation a decade later; or in 1969 when gay rights activists stood up against police at the Stonewall Tavern, giving birth to the gay rights movement that eventually brought greater protections for the LGBTQ community.

To many the 1886 Bay View Tragedy was a "loss" for the cause of workers. Coming one day after Chicago's Haymarket Affair, in which nine lost their lives, the two events were described in the newspapers as riots composed of thugs and anarchists, a characterization that tolled a temporary death knell to the nationwide campaign for an eight-hour workday.

Common to these worker and citizen revolts is the fact that at the time they were all "unpopular" in the public media and among the establishment. The Bay View marchers were called "rioters" and "thugs," even though they were mainly foundry and factory workers merely seeking a better life. Most were Polish and their lives were hardly valued with the establishment or the newspapers of the day; sounds similar to today's treatment of Hispanics and African Americans. Note also that virtually all those in the other solidarity movements of the last 150 years were called rioters, terrorists, anarchists, or "Commies."

All of this is understood by the few hundred people who show up each year at the Bay View Rolling Mills historic marker site. They're reminded that in the fight for justice there are often losses and sacrifices, but that if the oppressed continue to act in solidarity and perseverance, success will come.

That's why amidst the somber atmosphere in 2018, as we relived the grim history of May 5, 1886, through tears shed during the reading of the names of the seven victims, there is an obvious stirring of hope rising among the audience that comes from greeting old and new friends and allies in the struggle.

There have been no polls taken to show why hundreds show up each year. But my guess is that dedicated kindred spirits believe solidarity is still alive, and that it's time to dedicate themselves to the eternal fight for justice, at the workplace and in the community as a whole.

The Art of Labor:
A Tour of the Conflicted
Grohmann Museum

CALLEN HARTY

On Broadway in downtown Milwaukee, one might notice some tall bronze sculptures of burly men atop a building on the campus of the Milwaukee School of Engineering. The building is the home of the Grohmann Museum, an art museum dedicated to the exploration and study of men at work that opened in 2007. All of the artwork was donated by the immigrant industrialist Eckhart Grohmann, who collected it over a period of almost fifty years.

Having fought against Wisconsin Governor Scott Walker's assault on organized workers and having come from a working-class family of miners, house painters, farmers, and laborers, I had wanted to visit the museum since first seeing the sculptures from the street below. But it wasn't until a few years after the opening that I entered the museum, and left with conflicted feelings.

Upon entering the building you step into a light-filled glass entryway and see a floor with a pretty tiled mosaic by H. D. Tylle called "Men At Work." The mosaic depicts several trades embedded into the floor. There is a foundry worker, blacksmith, miner, farmer, and textile worker. You get the idea immediately that this place represents a celebration of labor, a paean to working men and women everywhere. Standing on the mosaic, you look up to see a brightly colored ceiling mural that shows Vulcan at his forge alongside Venus and Cupid. Elsewhere on the mural are depicted some of the world's great thinkers (Marie Curie, Thomas Edison, and Leonardo Da Vinci among them). Workers—whose labor is supposed to be celebrated here and whose labor helped those great thinkers achieve their places in our earthly pantheon—are on the floor beneath the feet of those who enter, tread upon as they strive to make the world a better place through their labor.

After touring the entire museum and upon further reflection, it struck me how the gods and thinkers were portrayed along with angels in the heavens above. On the floor, then, those who enter symbolically walk on the workers striving to earn a paycheck and make the world a better place. There were similar paradoxes throughout the museum, some enthralling and a few unsettling given the context of the benefactor's background, the fruits of labor and industry, and at least one of the featured artists.

As you go through the three floors of exhibits and the rooftop sculpture garden, most of the work you see is Eurocentric, with a heavy concentration of German artists represented. Upon learning that Grohmann was an immigrant from Germany in the early 1960s, this makes more sense. (That he was hardly alone in Milwaukee's place in German migration is worth noting, too.) Among the well-known names such as Peter Van Brueghel (the Younger) and Frederic Remington, many of the works are by unknown or lesser-known artists. Art critics may have an issue with the quality of the work, but again, given the focus of the museum on men at work, this, too, seems appropriate. Most of the laborers who toil day after day in factories and fields do so in obscurity while the captains of industry who employ them gain money and notoriety, so representations of laborers by obscure artists seems like an excellent egalitarian choice. But the choice is ultimately much more pedestrian than that. In an article on the opening of the museum in *On Milwaukee* (Ocober 30, 2007), Grohmann was quoted as saying, "I'm in the foundry business . . . I have a nuts-and-bolts background. I buy art based on subject matter, not who painted it." His intention is to show the evolution of work through his collection, not to showcase great artists (or perhaps even great art).

The museum does show men (and occasionally women) at work throughout history. While the artwork depicts laborers at their various trades, one has to keep in mind that the workers are not memorialized in the museum's name. Instead it is named after Grohmann, the German-American industrialist from Milwaukee who made his fortune off the backs of those laborers at an aluminum casting plant and other businesses in the Milwaukee area. In a January 2008 article in the *Wall Street Journal*, Grohmann talked about watching workers at his grandfather's quarry when he was a boy. "I loved to watch the guys." In various articles he talks about his fascination with the men who labor. And the *Wall Street Journal* article notes that "Dr. Grohmann never lost his respect for hard labor." (That feeling carries through in the museum's tagline, at least: ". . . the world's most comprehensive art collection dedicated to the evolution of human work.")

Then again, Grohmann made a fortune off that hard labor. In negotiations with the men whose work ethic he supposedly admired, the love seemed to get lost somewhere along the line. According to the website,

"Immigrant Entrepreneurship, German-American Business Biographies, 1720 to the Present," at one point Grohmann's "relationship with his over four hundred workers quickly deteriorated in disputes over working conditions, wages, and benefits." The article goes on to state that his foundry "gained a reputation among some in the surrounding South Side communities for its low pay and dangerous working conditions. Union organizers claimed ACE/CO's wages started at $5.85 per hour ($8.37 in 2010 US dollars), with many ACE/CO employees making $10 per hour ($14.30 in 2010 US dollars) or less. Grohmann strongly refutes these wage claims as little more than union propaganda. Contrary to the claims of union organizers, Grohmann asserts he did not run a sweatshop operation, but maintained tremendous respect for, and dedication to, his workers, compensating them accordingly." [Note: The $5.85 amount would be $9.66 in 2018 dollars.]

The article goes on to describe how employees who were concerned about pay and difficult working conditions banded together to form a new union which was voted in, but Grohmann refused to recognize it or negotiate with the workers. According to the immigrant entrepreneur website, the National Labor Relations Board later found Grohmann and his company guilty of several wrongdoings during the election of that union, "including denying workers their annual wage increase, giving preferential treatment to anti-union workers, and expressing its ambition 'to do everything possible' to remain union-free in its employee handbook." That sounds more like a man out to protect his own interests than a man who cares deeply about his workers. Perhaps he only loved those laborers who were willing to do his bidding without complaints or demands for economic justice.

A look at Grohmann's scant political contributions doesn't reflect a deep love of organized labor or worker justice. According to the Wisconsin Democracy campaign, Grohmann donated $2,500 between 1993 and 2011 to several of the more well-known anti-worker legislators campaigning in Wisconsin, including Mary Lazich, Alberta Darling, and Scott Fitzgerald.

There are many indications that Grohmann's love is not so much for labor but for the fruit of labor. In his museum there are paintings and sculptures that show men using tools to cut stone, harvest crops, make beer, and more. There are also works throughout that illustrate and celebrate the tools and machinery of labor over the laborers, paintings where things like lime kilns, bridges, and ships dominate the landscape and dwarf or obscure the workers who use or make them. At times it feels more like a celebration of industry, which uses labor to achieve its ends, rather than solely the examination of "men at work" that it purports to be.

Another issue, first brought to attention by the *Milwaukee Journal Sentinel* in an article by Mary Louise Schumacher and Whitney Gould in October 2007, has to do with three of the artists and their relationship to the Third Reich. One of those artists, Erich Mercker (1891-1973), "was commissioned directly by Hitler's government to create images of the Third Reich's expanding infrastructure," according to the newspaper. Of the 900 paintings and sculptures owned by the museum, more than eighty of Mercker's pieces are included. According to *Shepherd Express* (August 24, 2014), the Wolfsonian in Miami Beach is the only other museum in the United States that owns his work, and the only book about him was produced by the Milwaukee School of Engineering (MSOE).

In 2014 the museum featured a special exhibit of Mercker's work in which they acknowledged he was a member of the Nazi party. A *Milwaukee Journal Sentinel* article (December 5, 2014) quoted MSOE associate professor of history Patrick Jung as saying that in 2007, "the museum didn't know the extent of his participation with the Third Reich." Looking at his work with that knowledge, it becomes even clearer that his pieces glorifying German architecture, industry, and the like were used as propaganda even if that was not their intent. In addition, with many of the works in the museum created by several artists working under Hitler's regime, the countless shirtless, muscled men depicted seem less like physiques created from honorable labor than overwrought representations of supposed Aryan superiority. It seems an odd choice to have so many works represented by these artists.

Overall, the museum is all the more conflicting because of its fascinating elements. On the one hand you can see the worth of working men and women as they toil in their chosen fields. In painting after painting, sculpture after sculpture—in those in which the men (and, again, occasionally women) who do the work are depicted—you can see the dignity of working-class people. You can see the pride in their work, just as my father and his father had pride when they painted houses. The artists clearly admire them (in fact, as noted above, the depictions of the male laborers can make the museum seem more of a tribute to the beauty of the male form than to the male workers). The artists clearly celebrate the workers they show us. The nine-foot tall statues of laborers on the rooftop garden may seem like a gigantic tribute to the workers they represent, but the reality is that the statues are lifeless replicas. The museum as a whole appears to be a celebration of working-class heroes, but in the end the celebration seems to be more about the industrialist art collector who created the space and filled it with the things he liked best.

Perhaps a museum built by workers and housing works created by tradesmen and artists who have toiled in fields and factories would more likely be a celebration of working-class people. And the museum would not be named the Grohmann Museum. Instead, it would carry a name like The Art of Labor. I would gladly pay to tour such a place.

The Horseman in Lake Park

CARL A. SWANSON

A monument in Lake Park honors a man who once walked into a dwelling, pulled a knife, and sliced the homeowner wide open as he lay sprawled on his own kitchen table. When he left, he took one of the man's kidneys away with him.

There is more to the story . . .

The monument honors Erastus B. Wolcott, M.D., brilliant surgeon and benefactor of the poor. The emergency surgery described above took place on the patient's (well-scrubbed) kitchen table in 1861. The man survived the operation but died fifteen days later of exhaustion due to the difficult recovery. Still, Dr. Wolcott made medical history for performing the first-ever successful removal of a diseased kidney.

He was thirty-five when he arrived in Milwaukee on July 4, 1839. A graduate of the New York College of Physicians and Surgeons, Wolcott had previously served several years as an army surgeon stationed at Mackinac Island.

Early settler James S. Buck, writing in his four-volume *A Pioneer History of Milwaukee*, remembered the doctor as tall and slender, with light hair, kindly blue eyes, and a quick, emphatic way of speaking.

Other accounts describe the doctor's graceful manners, unusual in the pioneer community of 700 inhabitants but befitting a man whose family tree included six governors of the state of Connecticut plus a signer to the Declaration of Independence.

With his wife, Elizabeth Dousman Wolcott, and two children, the doctor lived in a house located where the Pfister Hotel now stands. He soon built a reputation as the territory's finest surgeon but Dr. Wolcott is chiefly remembered for his countless acts of charity. An article in the December 23, 1957, *Milwaukee Journal* noted, "He never formally billed his patients, and his devotion to them was boundless. He thought nothing of spending the night beside a sickbed. When he left at dawn, after a patient had fallen into a refreshing sleep—and if the family was a needy one—he was more than apt to place a dollar on the table holding the medicine so there would be milk and eggs for the patient and his family the next day."

In 1842, Dr. Wolcott became surgeon general of the territorial militia and, in 1846, major general of the Wisconsin militia. He served as manager of the state asylums for the insane and as a regent of the University of Wisconsin. He also had numerous business interests, including two early flour mills, and he was a key backer of the state's first railroad.

July 1849 is one of the darkest times in Milwaukee history. That month, six newly arrived immigrants died of cholera. Quickly the disease reached epidemic proportions. Day and night, wagons taking away the dead rolled through the city. Men, women, and children collapsed in the streets. Many of those stricken were abandoned to their fate by terrified family and friends. "And through it all," wrote Dr. Louis Frank in his 1915 *The Medical History of Milwaukee 1834-1914*, a history of early Milwaukee physicians, "moved Dr. Wolcott, tireless and unafraid, with potions for the suffering, at his side the noble Sisters of Mercy and Charity."

In 1857, Dr. Laura J. Ross arrived in the city. Just twenty-three years old, she was one of the first women in the United States to become a fully accredited M.D. She sought to join the local medical association but her application was opposed by most of Milwaukee's medical community—with the exception of Dr. Wolcott who advocated for her acceptance.

Strongly opposed to slavery, it was Dr. Wolcott who chaired the meeting called to protest the capture of runaway slave Joshua Glover, who was to be returned south to his slave owner under terms of the Fugitive Slave Act. Incensed Milwaukeeans broke into the city jail, freed Glover, and sent him on his way to safety in Canada.

Dr. Wolcott's wife, Elizabeth, died in 1860.

When the Civil War broke out the following year, Dr. Wolcott served with Wisconsin troops as surgeon general with the rank of brigadier and cared for the state's sick and wounded on many battlefields in that conflict. His statue in Lake Park depicts the doctor in his wartime uniform astride his favorite horse, Gunpowder.

Following the war, Dr. Laura Ross married Dr. Wolcott, thirty years her senior. She was active in women's rights and was instrumental in organizing major conventions in Milwaukee and in Madison in 1869, attended by Elizabeth Cady Stanton, Susan B. Anthony, and Mary A. Livermore.

In 1867, Dr. Wolcott became the first governor of the National Soldiers' Home (now the Milwaukee V.A. Medical Center) and led the initial development of the institution. One of the avenues running through the institution's grounds is named after him.

In January 1880, the doctor contracted acute pneumonia and died. He was seventy-six. In reporting the death, the *Milwaukee Sentinel* noted, "There is hardly a man, woman, or child in the city who did know the kindly face of the well-preserved old man, who had a pleasant word for all."

"Few men in the profession have performed as many and difficult surgical operations as has he. He was a born surgeon," wrote fellow pioneer James Buck. "Fearless himself, he soon infused the same spirit into others; his courage was undoubted and his coolness wonderful."

His wife continued to practice in Milwaukee until 1887, then moved to Philadelphia, and, finally, to a suburb of Chicago. She died in 1915. In her will she designated money for the statue of her husband in Lake Park. In a June 22, 1924, article, the *Milwaukee Journal* said the sculpture is significant for the nobility of its subject, its unusual pedestal, and its dramatic setting against a backdrop of trees. The article concluded, ". . . the statue is the gift of true affection. A wife, thinking of her own passing, did not plan to project her own personality beyond the grave but that of the man she loved."

The fifteen-foot, four-inch figure of the doctor astride his famous horse was designed by prominent sculptor Francis H. Packer. It is widely thought to be one of his finest works. The pedestal, bench, and terrace were designed by Albert Ross, who later oversaw construction of the Milwaukee County Courthouse. Originally the base included bronze eagles, also sculpted by Packer, at each end of the bench. The eagles were damaged by vandals in later years and removed.

Wolcott is the lone human sculpture tucked into Lake Park, a Frederick Law Olmsted gem in the string of Milwaukee County parks along Lake Michigan. Wolcott's statue is not as photographed as the Bronze Fonz, the TV tourist piece downtown, or as visible as Kosciuszko or Von Steuben, also atop horses as they face busy thoroughfares.

But Wolcott won't be soon forgotten. In 2007, with the monument showing the wear and tear of eight decades of Wisconsin weather, the Lake Park Friends raised more than $100,000 to have the statue and base restored.

The Wolcott monument was dedicated on June 12, 1920. Colonel Jerome A. Watrous, governor of the Wisconsin Veterans' Home, made the dedication speech and Mayor Daniel Hoan accepted the monument on behalf of the city. The inscription on the base, written by Colonel Watrois, reads:

Brigadier General Erastus B. Wolcott
Surgeon General of Wisconsin in Civil War and for thirteen years

afterward.
He lived a blameless life.
Eminent in his profession,
A lover of humanity,
Delighted to serve his fellow men, city, state and nation.

Novices

BRYAN JOHNSTON

I met her for the first time in the Emergency Department. It was early in my intern year in Milwaukee, back when I was still nervous to see patients alone. Her chest was heaving, she was drowning from the inside and could get out only a few gasping words, fluid thick around her lungs. She knew it was bad, she said, when she got back from the bathroom and just couldn't catch her breath. The fluid was everywhere else, too, veins blown out over the years, her body swollen like a sponge. The interview was brief, exam and workup obvious, plan straightforward. An IV was placed, medication started, and she settled onto our service. Progress was measured in kilograms, liters, oxygen requirements, daily reports of how deeply fingerprints indented her abdomen.

Eventually plans were made to send her home with a permanent port for IV diuretics and lab draws at home, which visiting nurses would push and pull on their visits. The attending physician shrugged when she left, something I have come to recognize as a response to the limits of medicine. I didn't know it then, but we would see her again soon.

Later that year I visited her at home. It was late fall and on the north side of Milwaukee, dry leaves collected in gutters and alleyways but snow had not yet come. She lived in a long line of identical, low apartment buildings, ten minutes from the hospital, or eight by ambulance.

I followed her doctor into a dark hallway where he knocked against and then opened the first door. We entered a modest and clean living room. I hesitated—I had never been inside a north side apartment before. I thought of myself as community-oriented. I taught nutrition at a nearby elementary school, I worked with the homeless and the uninsured, I'd been given awards for my community work, after all. But on the threshold I knew all of that meant nothing, was peripheral, existed in the domain of resumes.

I stepped on to the carpet, into the domain of real life. She lay in the corner of her bedroom, upright on an old hospital bed. Beside her a night stand contained a CPAP and mask, a phone charger, a host of pill bottles, and a large plastic cup of water—her 1.8 liter allotment for the day. I stood beside a small, bulbous television resting on several phone books while she talked with the doctor. I do not remember the conversation except that it was brief. I do not remember using the stethoscope or the blood pressure cuff.

I noticed a pair of green earphones by my foot, out of place in the apartment. Other signs of use—a child's bicycle helmet on the living room couch, dishes peeking above the kitchen sink—suggested the results of a careful cleaning operation, and that a dynamic life played out in this apartment when we were not expected. The blinds in her bedroom were down. She told us she kept them that way so she wouldn't catch herself missing the outdoors—she hadn't walked on her own down the steps to the curb in years. Her only travel was to and from the hospital, carried by burly emergency workers. In the car afterward, her doctor said she spends a lot of time watching television and thinking about how thirsty she is.

The next time I met her was in the hospital. The fluid was back, so much that she couldn't fit between the handles of her walker. This time it hadn't reached her lungs, though, and when I stopped by on my night rounds she invited me to sit and chat. She told me of her family, her past, stories weaving in and out of each other, ever growing. Her phone buzzed throughout our chat—"Let me call you back, the doctor's here," she would say, winking at me. Her room was a refuge for me that week, a bit of humanity in a night of lonely rounds through the quiet hospital hallways, furiously typed coverage notes which I knew no one would read, the feeling of treading water, waiting for one of the patients under my watch to crash. In our chats, I came to know a different person. Her doctor had offered her nursing home placement for years, and each time she declined. So hard to understand in the context of the helpless and ill patient, this was easier to grasp from the perspective of the matriarch, the provider, the lead actress in the story of her life.

A year and several admissions later, we were rounding when the code was called. She lay flat, compressions caving in her chest. The critical care doctor calmly directed the team of nurses and technicians from the foot of the bed. We edged in behind and urgently waited. The code stretched on. Then it was over and the room emptied all at once. I went back to the team room, the sound of grieving echoing throughout the unit. I know I am not the only one who still hears it.

The day finished routinely, somehow. I had plans that night, some frivolous thing or other, but found that I couldn't go. Some others felt the same, and we met up later at a bar down the street, pulling tables together as more and more residents arrived. Many had been welcomed into her home, all had been touched somehow in the process of caring for her. At first we were quiet and somber, but then the stories started. We felt proud. We had taken good care of her and she of us. It had taken creativity, coordination, and work to keep her with her family, her main goal, for so many years. We had helped her do it and that meant something. We toasted her, and before leaving poured 1.8 liters of water onto the sidewalk before each going off on our own, into the night. We are, in some ways, experts in the art of losing someone. In other ways we will always be novices.

"How Colorful My Life Has Become"

Four Essays from Students at St. Sava Orthodox School

Emily Meyer, English teacher at St. Sava Orthodox School in Milwaukee, collected essays from her fifth to eighth grade students in spring 2018 to help share the perspectives of her Serbian (and in one case, Russian) students who are first-, second- and third-generation emigres to the United States. As she described the school and students, "The class sizes range from three to eight students, so quite small! . . . The students speak Serbian and English fluently. Many of them begin school in 4K not knowing any English, and by eighth grade a good number of students graduate going on to Honors English in high school. I should also note that I am not Serbian—in fact only the principal/math teacher and the Serbian language teacher are from Serbia."

"The students who attend here are quite confident in where they came from and there is a real sense of family here. We honor their Serbian Orthodox traditions . . . and respect their family's life stories. We are a school just like any other—we are a team of dedicated teachers who want the best for our students."

Below are essays from four of those grade-school students in Meyer's English classes.

DANICA TRIVUNOVIC

Hello my name is Danica and my parents are from Europe. My dad's from Bugojno, Bosnia and my mom is from Banatski Despotovac, Serbia. My parents chose to live in Milwaukee because of the war.

War in Bosnia started in 1992. The civil war was a really dangerous war for citizens in Bosnia. My dad was only fourteen-years old when the war was happening. Being a refugee from the war in Bosnia, my dad, his sister, and his mom left Bosnia, and went to Serbia. When my mom and dad met in Serbia, they fell in love. They dated for six years and got married in Serbia. In the meantime, my dad got visas to come to America.

On May 22, 2003, my dad came to America with my grandma without my mom. From that day on my dad started a new life from being a refugee in the war. My grandma and dad rented an apartment near our church, St. Sava. Many people from Bosnia moved to America. Since my grandma knew some people in America, those people helped my dad and grandma get a job in Milwaukee. My dad got a job at Pillar Induction and after fourteen years he's still working there. Since my dad had his visa, he started filling out papers for my mom so that she could move here, too. After seventeen months passed, my mom came to America. Two months later, my mom got a job at Eder Flag company. Thirteen years later my mom still works there as a supervisor.

When I asked my parents why they moved to Wisconsin they said it was because of a better opportunity to succeed. Milwaukee is a big city, with many places to go. We like to spend a lot of time near Lake Michigan. We have many memories in Wisconsin. Deciding which school should my sister and I go to, my parents said St. Sava Orthodox School. St. Sava has wonderful teachers and provides my sister and I with good education. For my parents it is really important to keep the Serbian tradition, to learn the Serbian language and to read Serbian. In St. Sava, there aren't many students, but we all know each other. My parents met my friends' parents at church and school celebrations. Since we don't have many relatives here, our friends mean a lot to us.

My experience with being a student in St. Sava school is wonderful. Wearing school uniforms we all look the same, no rich or poor students. And every school year I was part of a play which created a lot of good memories and fun with my friends. Lastly, in our kitchen we have delicious smells coming from the kitchen everyday. Everyday they cook Serbian traditional foods. Being a student in St. Sava, I am very proud and happy to meet all the wonderful teachers and a lot of good friends.

ANA JURIC

Being the firstborn of my Serbian Orthodox family, I have a salient responsibility to carry on our traditions. I take on the role to teach my brother and sister about our faith and origin. One of the honorable customs in Orthodoxy is the Slava. I find this tradition significant because it shows how much we cherish our faith.

Slava is a yearly celebration executed by all Orthodox families in which they have a feast in their home and invite other family members in honor of a saint. Each saint has a day of the year that they are celebrated as well. For instance, my family and I have Saint Stefan. Every year we prepare food for January 9th, which is the day he is celebrated, and await guests to come honor our saint. Families generally carry different slavas, but it is often the case where some families share the same saint's day. As a religious family that celebrates the Slava, it is important to remember why we are doing so. The Slava brings worship and remembrance to the saints, as well as bringing love and togetherness to our family, which altogether, reinforces our faith. I am honored and delighted to teach the significance of Slava to my siblings and to pass on the glorified tradition to the following generations.

Not only is my culture fascinating, but so are the life stories of my parents. They were both mainly raised in Bosnia and the war had a major effect on their lives. My mother grew up on a farm helping her mother while her father fought in the army. It was hard for her to grow up knowing her dad was risking his life every day. My father, on the other hand, spent his week days in school in Belgrade and came home to the country to his grandparents over the weekends. The war did not affect his life as much as it did my mother's, but it still pushed him to the decision to move to America.

Choosing where in the United States to start a new life was a tough decision. He ended up choosing Milwaukee because most of his family was there and it had a well-respected Serbian Orthodox Church where he promised to continue his traditions as a Serb. My father flew to his new life from Belgrade while my mother was still jumping from place to place around Europe. My mom and her family moved a lot to escape the war and eventually ended up in Croatia. From there, they got their papers and were able to go to Milwaukee. My mother's main reason why she chose Milwaukee was because of family. Her uncle was a priest at the Serbian Orthodox Church in Milwaukee and they couldn't wait to reunite. My parents met in Milwaukee and bonded over their similarities associating with their lives in Bosnia. Soon, they were married and had three kids . . .

We proudly continue our Serbian customs here in Milwaukee. One of the traditions that is executed by most Serbs in the United States is Serbian Folk Dancing (or Folklore). Folklore groups all over the United States are learning dances that were constructed around the nineteenth century and they perform them annually in traditional Folklore costumes. These costumes were worn daily in Serbia centuries ago and are now mainly used for performances. I am honored to put forth that I participate in my own Serbian community's Folklore group, which has over 200 members. We learn new dances and choreograph them in time for each performance.

Performing these dances in honor of our history fills my heart with joy. The amount of love that has blossomed in my heart for my religion and culture while growing up in Milwaukee is truly admirable and I cannot possibly put into words how colorful my life has become because of it.

DUSAN BRANKOV

Hi, my name is Dusan and I am a Serbian kid with two brothers. My parents chose to live in Milwaukee. My dad is from Kikinda, Serbia, but was born in Australia, and my mom is from Zenica, Bosnia. My dad left Serbia because he wanted to study in America, and my mom left her home because she was fleeing from war. My dad chose to live in Milwaukee because he had cousins that lived in Milwaukee who had called him to live with them. My mom chose to live in Milwaukee because her brother lived here and because she met and fell for my dad.

I was born in West Allis in February 2007. Milwaukee is one of the best places to live. For one, you can't drive a half mile and not run into some restaurant or frozen custard shop. Also, I read that Milwaukee is the home of the most frozen custard and ice cream shops in the area.

My first day at St. Sava Orthodox School was in September 2011. My first day, like a lot of other first days, was bad. I kept crying and wailing and wanting for my mom to come back and get me. But after a while, I quit doing it. My other years were all pretty good, and school was becoming a breeze.

Anyway, I have lived in Milwaukee for eleven years, so I know it like the back of my hand (sort of). I have always enjoyed going with my dad to see Milwaukee, like going to stores or places for auto parts. Each time I went with Dad, I saw a new part of Milwaukee that gets implanted in my brain. That's not all. I go to downtown Milwaukee very often during the summer, and the sights there are amazing. Every time I go, we spend some time eating Potbelly sandwiches and watching other kids run through the water fountains. I will always love and appreciate Milwaukee, for it is the best place to live. But I think that Milwaukee won't always be my home, because my parents want us to move and live in Greendale or Russia. But Milwaukee is still the best place I have ever lived.

NASTASJA RADULOVIC

My name is Nastasja. I am half Bulgarian, and half Serbian. My mother is Bulgarian, and my father is Serbian. My mother came to America when she was 22, with only $100. Her first job was as a waitress in Wisconsin Dells. My father was born in Kenosha. My father was second generation, the first being my grandparents. Both grandparents being from Bosnia—my grandmother was from Doboj, and my grandfather was Gornja Slatina. My father's side is in America, or are still in Bosnia and Herzegovina. My Bulgarian family is mainly located in Bulgaria, however I have cousins in Italy.

The main reason my parents chose to move to Milwaukee was to find good jobs. My father was born and raised in Racine County. For both my mother and father, Milwaukee had better jobs than Racine County. There were better medical fields to work in Milwaukee and better positions for engineering . . .

Growing up in a Serbian community has greatly affected me. I've grown to understand the Serbian community, how I am surrounded with its language, people, and food. I have been part of a Serbian Cultural Dance Group since I was three. Milwaukee has an immense Serbian community. In Milwaukee, I attend St. Sava Orthodox School. This school is one of two schools that is Serbian Orthodox in all of America. The school also provides a Serbian language class to learn Serbian. The Serbian class helps to understand and communicate with grandparents, or acquaintances that do not know English as well as others might.

I believe it is very important to know the language of your history. It brings a closer connection to me and my family. Going to St. Sava gave me the opportunity to make friends in the same culture as I am. With friends of the same culture, you can connect easier, and have more things in common.

The Clarke Street School Playground

FRANCES ASSA

Clarke Street School, and its playground, was the center of my life, and of the neighborhood, which ran from about North Avenue to Burleigh, and Twenty-fifth to Thirtieth Streets.

Like many of the school's parents in the 1950s, mine were immigrants from Europe. My classmates often had German, Ukrainian, or Serbian names, some unpronounceable. Ugljesha quickly became "Yogi," after the cartoon bear on TV. People were immigrating to Milwaukee because things were booming. A. O. Smith, with its new all-glass building on Twenty-seventh and Capitol, was hiring and paid good union wages. Miller Brewery was not far away.

Every day I walked to school from our home behind our grocery store on Twenty-ninth and Wright. My mother ran the store, and from age ten I helped out behind the counter, working the cash register and selling loaves of Wonder Bread, quarts of milk, and packages of unfiltered cigarettes for twenty-five cents each. In fifth grade we moved to a store north of the Center Street and Fond du Lac Avenue commercial intersection, where the library was. In the winter, on our way home from school, my friends and I would duck into Woolworth's to warm up and watch the parakeets and tiny turtles.

The school building and the neighborhood were old even then. Despite this, the run-down, clapboard houses were teeming with children. We were the baby boomers, and one summer, trucks and workers arrived to expand the Clark Street School playground, covering the rest of the city block in asphalt in order to accommodate us. After school, we roller-skated on rough, uneven sidewalks with steel skates that attached to our shoes with keys, but now it was a treat to skate on the new smooth asphalt of the playground. Bicycles were for the kids of middle-class neighborhoods farther west, near Sherman and Washington Parks, literally on the other side of the tracks at Thirtieth Street. That was another world. We would meet them years later at one of the junior high schools, or at Washington High School, a pinnacle of learning in the city.

In the evenings, the school offered activities for both adults and children, and a Brownies troop. Sometimes, while skating, I'd see the

Brownies gather on the playground. The Brownie leader let on to my mother, who had a thick German accent, that there was a Jewish girl who wanted to join, but she would make sure that that never happened, not knowing that she was talking to that Jewish girl's mother. I was the only Jew in the school and proudly stood silent during the more religious Christmas carols we sang throughout December.

Strangely enough, in this all-white environment, we had an African American fourth grade teacher, Mrs. Dorothy Carter, whom we adored. She must have been a rarity at Milwaukee Public Schools at the time. Googling her a few years ago, I learned that she had been a graduate of Spelman College, had studied drama in New York under Stella Adler, Marlon Brando's teacher, and had appeared on Broadway in *Strange Fruit* (1945) and *Take a Giant Step* (1953.) After her stint at Clarke Street School, she was appointed Milwaukee Elementary Curriculum Supervisor, served as an instructor at the University of Wisconsin, and then taught at the prestigious Bank Street College in New York while obtaining a doctorate at Teachers College, Columbia University. In retirement, Carter directed plays for the Morningside Theater in New York, and had three children's books published that told of growing up in a small segregated southern town.

Through Dorothy Carter, and the school building itself, we were exposed to excellence and beauty. The building was an old Victorian pile with pointed roofs. It had a soaring entranceway graced with a grand staircase that was lit by a great Palladian window, and it gave me a lifelong interest in architecture.

But my heart was at the playground. Tall, and with long legs, I gained physical confidence and proceeded to beat everyone I could at kickball and dodgeball. Mrs. Carter instilled me with confidence in my mind, too, when she smiled and nodded approvingly at my answer to her question about what I wanted to be when I grew up. I told her I planned to discover the cure for cancer.

Today, the houses that were deteriorating when we lived in them, are now sixty years older. The waves of European immigrants of my day, were soon replaced by waves of African Americans seeking better-paying work. Now the factories are gone, and the neighborhood is poorer than ever. Many houses are shuttered and literally falling down. Grass fills many lots where houses once stood.

I visited the Clark Street School recently. The grand entry hall seems smaller but it is even more beautiful. Like the rest of the school it is filled with marvelous artwork. Huge, brightly painted *papier-mâché* wild animals tread the stairs. Inside, I am greeted by the adults, and even a few of the children, who look more excited to be there than we were. Where we were all white, the children now are all black, and the schools are as segregated as they were in the early sixties. Blackboards have become obsolete, but segregation has not.

I had come to drop off a package. I wanted to make a small donation to the school and had called the principal to find out what she might want. She was delighted and immediately replied: "pencils." I had supposed she'd ask for something more exotic. Evidently students are expected to supply their own pencils, but often can't afford to, so teachers pay for such things out of their own pockets. When I was a child all school supplies were provided. We as a society are unable to provide even pencils to our poorest children.

A lack of pencils, of course, is not the biggest tragedy. That occurred one summer evening in 2014 when ten-year-old Sierra Guyton was playing on the Clarke Street School playground. Was she roller skating when it happened? I don't know. She was caught in the crossfire of a shooting incident, shot three times, and died of her wounds a few days later.

From Kanty

JIM KOGUTKIEWICZ

Thirty-two years before they shut down my South Side church, I was a new altar boy serving his first Sunday Mass and dutifully following the instructions of Father Jim Winiarski, the associate pastor at Saint John Kanty at the time in the 1980s. A few weeks earlier, Father Carl Kazmierczak, the pastor at Saint John Kanty, had come to my third-grade class looking for new altar boys, and I flashed my arm toward the heavens—a bolt of lightning in reverse—to volunteer to serve. I had been dreaming about it since I started school, so this first Mass, for a respectful Polish boy who grew up half a block from the altar, was a moment overflowing with anticipation. And Father Jim, who appeared to be twice our height and always smiled kindly behind prominent cheeks and twinkling eyes, had a special instruction for me in the sacristy before we started: when the Pope arrived, I needed to "give him the signal" so he could welcome John Paul II himself to our Sunday service on Dakota Avenue between Ninth Place and Tenth Street. Father Jim would be far too busy saying the Mass, of course, to watch the back door to see if the Popemobile—his exact word choice—had pulled up along the curb. But if I just alerted him to the Pope's arrival ASAP, all would be well.

To that point, I'd been consumed by fear of kneeling at the wrong time or ringing the bells during consecration with too much vigor. Now I had to keep an eye out for the Pope, too. It made me sweat with fear under my cassock. Prior to consecration, when we poured water over the priest's hands to wash them, Father Jim bent in half at the waist to lean down toward us, and he whispered to me, "Any sign of the Pope?"

My GOD! This was for real! I told Father Jim I had not yet seen the Pope. To my amazement, he shrugged it off, dried his hands, and went ahead with the Mass. The Pope was late for Mass, and Father Jim seemed entirely unperturbed, but I stayed vigilant and kept my eyes glued to the back door, oblivious to the dozens of people sitting in the pews. They were my neighbors, classmates, and parents of friends. They were the only people in the world as I knew it in the flesh, basically, and they consisted wholly of people from a few blocks in either direction of the church. And until Father Jim talked to me, I had been scared of looking silly in front of them. Now I was struggling to register how I would handle a face-to-face meeting with the supreme pontiff.

Father Jim didn't continue the act for long after Mass ended. I believe he again shrugged off the Pope's non-appearance and just left to go about his day. I, however, ended up serving as an altar boy through eighth grade and even into my high school years.

On September 8, 2018, I finally did see Pope John Paul II at Saint John Kanty. His large portrait, in an ornate gold frame, was on display in an alcove on the west wall. As part of the decommissioning Mass marking the closing of the 111-year-old church, it was taken down from its display under lights and held aloft by a parishioner. The image of the Polish Pope, his hands folded in prayer, a slight smile on his face as he gazed to the distance, obscured the body and head of the man holding it. It looked as though the deceased Pope had put on a pair of black slacks and shoes to stop in and honor the church's legacy.

The decommissioning was necessary because the church's boiler finally gave out and there was no money to replace it. Once winter set in, the building would be effectively unusable, so the Archdiocese of Milwaukee decided to sell the nearly full city block of land that the church and school occupied since 1907. The church was the second one built on that plot of land, replacing the original structure that was immediately to the west of it. The two buildings that housed the school were an older, two-story sandy-red brick one for grades up through four, and then a flat, one-story cream-colored brick-and-glass building on the north side of the block for grades five through eight. It all was up for sale.

I sat in the pew at the decommissioning next to my mom, a single mother who raised me in the house she grew up in on Ninth Place between Dakota and Manitoba Avenues. We lived in the cozy upper unit of the South Side duplex, and my grandma—my mother's mom—lived downstairs. During that final Mass, in the church that served as the center of my upbringing, my mother's life, and the life of my late grandmother, my mind drifted through the memories while the rhythms of the Catholic Mass played out. Some of the words and phrases had changed, but all the familiar beats of my youth remained, and the memories popped back for me to reconsider.

Saint John Kanty church looks as though someone had placed a three-story letter "A" in the heart of a South Side Milwaukee neighborhood. Inside, the stations of the cross ringed the short walls, and above that, the ceiling on each side sloped dramatically upward to form that A-shape, covered in repeating crest designs that always reminded me of something out of *The Three Musketeers*. This was the place I trudged to on frigid, dark winter mornings to serve at 6:45 a.m. Mass. The week I had that assignment meant I could show up at the very end of the mandatory 8:00 a.m. Mass all children at Saint John Kanty were required to attend before school started each day. It was among these pews I had anxiously counted down the lighting of so many purple advent candles in anticipation of Christmas, observed feasts of the Immaculate Conception, served as an altar boy at a funeral attended by one person, trembled before entering the confessional for the sacrament of Reconciliation, and once even asked my mom and grandma if we could stay longer after a service because I felt I had not prayed enough to God to protect them. And in a less pure example of such devotion, it was here that as a teenager I received the sacrament of Confirmation and chose the name Sidney for the ceremony. Ostensibly, this was to take the name of the Blessed Sidney Hodgson, martyred in London in 1591, but in reality it was to sneak in an official church recognition that I'd taken the same name as Sidney Moncrief, my favorite player on the Milwaukee Bucks. It was a ceremony that marked my progression to the next step of my faith, which ended up becoming "I was RAISED Catholic."

Even decades later, I suppose, we feel compelled to confess.

The community that surrounded this place of such intense experiences was small. Oklahoma Avenue is two blocks to the south of Saint John Kanty, but it served as a kind of Great Wall of Catholics during my childhood. Saint Helen's church and school was two blocks south of that, on Tenth Street, and everybody who attended Helen's south of Oklahoma Avenue was practically from another country. One of the closest friends I've ever had grew up two blocks away from me and attended Saint Helen's. But we lived on either side of Oklahoma Avenue, so I didn't meet him until freshman football practice at Saint Thomas More High School. How did we break down this Catholic neighborhood upbringing? "You went to Kanty's, right?" he said while we ran laps around the school's track. That was all it took to knock down the two-block divide between our houses, but talking to him before that was unthinkable.

Further to the west was Saint Alexander's church and school on Sixteenth Street between Ohio and Holt Avenues. Only a mile away from my boyhood home, it might as well have been the Moab Desert for a kid from Saint John Kanty. I only knew one kid growing up, almost by accident, who was from Saint Alexander—you were always "from" a church in those days, not someone who merely attended it.

For some time now, Saints Alexander, Helen, and John Kanty churches have been combined as Saint John Paul II parish, with the trio being considered one congregation with three "campuses" so to speak. The failing boiler at Saint John Kanty drops that number to two, which is a shock for someone who feels indelibly shaped for the good by the Catholic traditions, education, and values that marked my family and my way of life. Sure, I grew up and away from the church as I aged, but the constancy of Saint John Kanty, which my mom faithfully attended to the very end of its existence, was the foundation for everything.

But now I'm teetering on the edge of taking myself too seriously. As the "Pope Watch" lesson from Father Jim taught me, not every moment in the church needs to be handled with sacred grace. Flashing back through the memories of my time as an altar boy, I realize Father Jim's dry sense of humor also revealed to me a secret world of adults that they didn't display for obedient altar boys and other churchgoing children. Father Jim showed me how hilarious that could be one Sunday morning in the sacristy, a room where the priest prepared for Mass. At Saint John Kanty, it was immediately off the altar to the west side of the building—in theater terms, it was "stage right." The room contained religious artifacts and priests' garments kept in blonde wood cabinets against one wall. The sacristy floor was a royal red carpet that was well worn, but always struck me as conveying importance and sanctity. No families I knew had such a deeply red floor anywhere in their house, and if it's in the church and not found anywhere else, it's automatically holy, even if it's just carpet.

Before one Sunday Mass, in the sacristy with the sacred red carpet, Father Jim became the first authority figure I ever saw in my life casually swear in front of me. He delivered the shocking obscenity with such perfect tone that I've remembered it in my mind's eye ever since. You see, Saint John Kanty had a church organist at the time named Marilyn Selendek. She was a short, stout woman with an unmistakable voice that boomed at all times. She also was the music teacher in the school, though her classes consisted of mostly sing-alongs for half an hour—I can still blurt out the chorus to "Mr. Touchdown" on command. Naturally, you might conclude that eleven- and twelve-year-olds in 1987 might not fill with joy while being forced at piano-point to sing college football fight songs from the era of raccoon coats and rabid pennant waving. Your conclusion would be correct, and Marilyn Selendek responded to our musical indifference, on occasion, with impotent shouting that we'd better sing along if we knew what was good for us.

Her tone was more measured when preparing for Sunday Mass, but everybody experienced the same version of Marilyn Selendek. One particular Sunday, she had called the sacristy using the direct-line phone that served as a sort of hotline from the organ and choir in the balcony above the altar. She had some things to say about how the music during the service would be coordinated, and I sat in a chair next to the phone while Father Jim listened, expressionless. He mumbled a couple agreeing "Uh, huhs" to Marilyn during the call, and then ended their exchange by telling her that he was really looking forward to a movie that was going to be on TV that night. It was called *Bitch and Moan, Bitch and Moan: The Marilyn Selendek Story.*

Then he hung up the phone, gathered the altar boys and volunteer parishoners who would do the readings at Mass and we hit the floor, ready to start the show. The sacristy had crackled for a second after he delivered the line, but Father Jim played it in a perfect deadpan. He knew it was good, so he didn't have to sell the joke. He went right back to being the associate pastor of Saint John Kanty who was leading the congregation in the celebration of Sunday Mass. All these years later, it's still exciting to think about a priest laying a bomb on somebody like that.

Father Jim was soon given his own parish, on Howell Avenue out by General Mitchell International Airport, close to the border with Oak Creek. I'm not sure where he ended up, but if I could ever talk to him again, I'd thank him for showing me that an authority figure could be a responsible adult even though he swore in front of a kid. And I'd shake his hand twice as hard in appreciation for giving me a priceless lesson in selling a joke.

While Father Jim was a favorite, no priest that passed through Saint John Kanty during my childhood came across like a genuine buddy as did Father Jeremy. As the pastor, Father Carl always seemed too stern and humorless to the kids in school. (He was known, quite cruelly, as Gargamel for his vague resemblance to the lead villain from *The Smurfs*.) And Father Jim, for all his genius with a joke, still understood he was a leader and in a position that required a certain distance.

But Father Jeremy was younger and had no hard edges. His round, full face displayed understanding and kindness. He was shorter than the other priests, more on our physical level as altar boys, and had a slight paunch. He wore a bushy mustache and had dark, thick hair combed that way all men in the eighties could wear a simple side part that looked impossibly full, like a hair helmet. Father Jeremy was immensely likeable and I admired him. Any Mass he celebrated offered a chance for a more inspiring, even fun experience in church.

So when Father Jeremy told me he was hosting a party for the altar boys from Saint John Kanty, it seemed too good to be true. My mom, however, was less thrilled. The whole thing sounded fishy to her, and in retrospect, it's easy to see why. But I was desperate to attend. My favorite priest holding a party for all the altar boys on a weekend afternoon. I pleaded with my mom to say it was okay to go, but she needed proof that what was happening was actually happening. So one Sunday shortly before the party, fully embarrassed and unable to hardly even look at him, I told Father Jeremy in the sacristy that my mom wanted him to send home a letter with me that explained he actually was having this party and that everything would be supervised and okay. I was mortified that my mother was expressing doubt and that Father Jeremy needed to prove my story.

Without hesitation, and in his perfectly calm, kind manner, Father Jeremy said of course he would send such a letter home with me. He told me to follow him into the Saint John Kanty rectory, and the two of us walked the hundred or so feet from the church to the church's house for the pastor. Inside he sat down at a typewriter, and on Saint John Kanty letterhead, typed up a brief note explaining when and where this party for altar boys would take place, and gave my mom all the assurance she needed. I took it home, and it satisfied her. I could attend the party.

The decommissioning of Saint John Kanty—and all the literal and symbolic summing up that it entailed—brought back these memories of Father Jeremy because of all my experiences, this party and what it became remain an unresolved question about my upbringing in this tight-knit Polish South Side neighborhood.

The events from the day of the party were so flat, dull, and weird that I've questioned my own recollections of it at times. What remains clear in my head is that Father Jeremy said we would all watch a movie, and at some point I went with him, alone, to a local video rental store and there was some joking small talk with the clerks there. At one point he patted my head. Then we went to his residence on Howard Avenue near the city limits by Saint Francis. It was a brown apartment building on a corner, and inside there were a bunch of altar boys sitting around on the floor. Father Jeremy started the movie—I vaguely recall it being *Day of the Dolphin*, which, I mean, come on—and everyone was just mindlessly bored. The room was dark, and Father Jeremy seemed intent on watching the movie while all the boys gradually realized nothing approaching fun would happen that day. And this party became just sitting around doing not much of anything with a priest.

In thinking back to this party every once in a while, nothing beyond what's been recounted here has ever come to mind. And I recall, clearly, my fondness for Father Jeremy remaining after the party and all the way through his sudden announcement that he would be leaving the area and going to serve a mission in Madagascar. I had to find Madagascar on the globe in our classroom, because I'd certainly never heard of it before. The news devastated me. As a child of a single mom raised by two women, father figures were few and far between. Father Jeremy was someone I looked up to and enjoyed being around, a person who was gentle and understood life. He announced the mission to the congregation at Mass one week and that was it. I don't recall seeing him after that.

As I grew up through the nineties and the Catholic Church in America was forced to deal with its legacy of covered-up abuses, sometimes I wondered about that party, the strangeness of it. A priest sitting around in a darkened room with a bunch of boys watching a movie. As the Archdiocese of Milwaukee's own tragedy of covered-up abuses under Archbishop Rembert Weakland came to light, I eventually read stories about victims from Milwaukee and how things were covered up. I even once specifically looked for Father Jeremy's name in a list, though I couldn't remember his last name. Regardless, I never found anyone named Jeremy among Catholic priests from Milwaukee known to have abused children, though in fairness to all concerned, I only looked one time and would be honest enough, now, to admit I hoped I would not find one.

As I went through adolescence and moved on to college at UW-Milwaukee, I drifted away from the church. It was also during this time that my grandma started to slip. Her dementia developed over a long period, and this woman possibly leaving us presented too many emotional burdens for me. She'd taken a boat to America as a child, told us she learned to speak English at a school on Muskego Avenue near Mitchell Street, and spoke of the difficulties endured and overcome during the Great Depression with a dignified pride—surviving that ordeal meant everything to her. To cope with facing the loss of such a powerful, proud matriarch, I used a joking tone with her much of the time. As a teenager and even into my early twenties, she might ask me where I was heading as I would make my way out of the house. "I'm going to St. Louis, grandma. I'll be back later." I always told her I was on my way to St. Louis. She would laugh and smile with love, seemingly pleased her grandson was a jokester and willing to kid with her.

But one day around this time, in the kitchen at the back of the house, with the antique framed print of *The Last Supper* hanging over the breakfast nook windows, she stood in the doorway leading out toward the backyard and was looking around for something. I was standing a few feet away, on the opposite side of the round wooden table that sat in the middle of kitchen. Using the same tone of voice that brought a smile to her face when joking about road trips to St. Louis, I asked, "Whatcha looking for, Grandma?"

She paused for a beat or two, looking down and away toward the floor. She brought her eyes to mine and a smile of resigned acceptance came across her face; she had lost her train of thought from a moment earlier and knew it. But she still told me what she was looking for.

"Time," she said, and let out the slightest half-breath of a sigh.

At my grandma's funeral a few years later, my mom made sure the home handling the services led the procession from Saint John Kanty south on Ninth Place and past our house. The funeral director hemmed and hawed a bit, saying the procession usually heads for the cemetery up Tenth Street and toward Oklahoma Avenue, but my mom insisted and he led everyone up Ninth Place instead, like Grandma wanted. One last trip home from church.

Ironically, the decommissioning Mass ended with a walking procession from Saint John Kanty—along Tenth Street—to Saint Helen's four blocks south. It was a ceremonial end to signify that though the building was closing, the congregation would live on at the other two locations for the parish. We lingered a bit after Mass and fell far behind the procession. We hurried up Tenth Street for a block to try and catch up, but we were too far behind and abandoned the effort. Besides, home was on Ninth Place. Grandma had done it right.

IN PERSON

We Got This

JAMES E. CAUSEY

It's 5:15 a.m. on Monday August 13, 2018, and Arthur Ellis, a black man with salt and pepper hair, is already on his knees, meditating in front of twenty-four, four-by-six-foot vegetable gardens on a lot on North Ninth and Ring Streets in Milwaukee.

Even though it's early, the block is eerily quiet.

The only thing that can be heard on this sunny morning are cardinals chirping in a nearby blackberry bush that is full of juicy ripe black fruit.

The man's eyes are closed and his hands are clasped together as he sits on a green wooden bench. The sun is beaming off his face and the white 53206 embroidered on his black baseball hat provides contrast against the lush green background.

The 53206 ZIP code is an area bounded by Interstate 43 to the east, Twenty-seventh Street to the west, North Avenue to the south, and Capitol Drive to the north. A 2015 documentary, *MILWAUKEE 53206,* labeled the ZIP code as the most incarcerated area in America. Crime statistics show that the homicide rate in 53206 is 250 per 100,000, well above the nation's rate of 4.9 per 100,000.

For all the negative that the media reports on the area, Ellis is working tirelessly as an advocate for change.

His "We Got This" mentoring program, which started in 2014, teaches black boys ages twelve to sixteen not only gardening skills, but how to be responsible neighbors and good men. After cleaning up the neighborhood, the boys get personal group time with their adult male mentors, something many don't get to see daily.

The program has received national acclaim and has even drawn the attention of comedian and talk show host Steve Harvey, who named Ellis a "Harvey's Hero." Harvey presented Ellis with a $10,000 Green Dot gift card when he had him on the show in January 2016.

Ellis moved into the area in December 2011 due to finances. "It was the only place we could afford," he said.

"When we moved over here I just kept asking my wife why things were so bad. Why were drug dealers selling drugs right across the street from the school? Why were there gunshots being fired every night? Why were kids fighting in the streets? Why didn't anyone seem to care?"

On his fifth day living on the block, Ellis was coming from the corner grocery store when six shots rang out. He ran into his house and his wife Angela checked to see if he had been hit. A man lay dead in the street. Ellis remembers the yellow tape that went up around the body. He remembers the families arriving at the scene, breaking down in tears and screaming as the police tried to question potential witnesses.

He also remembers looking at an empty lot and seeing a pile of dirt in the middle of it. He asked what it was supposed to be and a young boy told him that it was supposed to be a community garden but nobody ever did anything with it.

At that point Ellis declared, "shit had to change," and he was going to lead the charge.

He found out who owned the lot and eventually purchased it and moved to turn it into a community garden because there were no full service grocery stores in the area.

Being a fly on the wall on a block that had open air drug dealing across the street from a middle school was not something Ellis could tolerate.

So he put his acting skills to the test.

One morning when a dealer was selling cocaine on the corner, Ellis walked up to the man and asked him his name. The drug dealer gave him an alias.

Ellis took out a piece a paper from his back pocket, looked at it, and said, "You're the guy the police were talking about at the community meeting last night. They are looking for you."

The next day the drug dealer was gone.

"You can either be an active participant and try to fix things or stand on the sidelines and watch things fail and do nothing," Ellis said. "Anybody who knows me will tell you that I'm a fighter. And I'm not talking about owning a gun. I'm talking about fighting for these kids. This is a matter of life and death."

Ellis worked his plan for the next two to three summers before the garden would be ready.

When he got the garden set up, he didn't really know what to do next.

Then something happened on a July day in 2014. Around 3:30 p.m. someone was pounding on Ellis's front door like the police. When he went to the door it was a woman. She was hysterical. She told Ellis that the police took her son, Jermaine, into custody for breaking into people's cars in the neighborhood.

Ellis asked her what she wanted him to do about it and she told him that he was her only hope.

"You say you want to help the youth, then help my son," she told him.

As she began to cry, Ellis asked her where Jermaine's father was and she told him that he left her before Jermaine was even walking.

"I saw the pain in her eyes and I told her don't worry, we got this," Ellis said.

When he went down to the Fifth District Police station, he was well known because of the positive work he had done on his block in getting neighbors and police involved. He talked with the lieutenant about Jermaine and told him that he had a program he just started that Jermaine was going to be a part of next week.

Ellis made up the idea for the program on the spot. He called it "We Got This" and said Jermaine was going to work for him for four hours, cleaning up the streets and learning how to garden. He said Jermaine was going to be paid $20 for four hours of work.

Jermaine was released into Ellis's custody that night and Ellis told him that next week he had to be at the garden at 8:00 a.m. prepared to work or that he was done with him.

The following week, Jermaine arrived at 7:15 a.m. Ellis made him work, putting down topsoil and picking up bags of trash throughout the neighborhood. Jermaine didn't give any backtalk and did everything Ellis asked.

During his break, Jermaine said, "Mr. Andre, I'm not as bad as people say. But the people around me who tell me to do right are doing things worse than me."

Ellis paid Jermaine $20 and told him to come back next week.

Later that day, when Ellis was coming from the store with his wife, he saw a young man wearing white jeans and a white shirt.

"I said baby, look at that boy right there, he's sharp. I did a double take and it was Jermaine."

Ellis stopped his car and asked Jermaine what he was so happy about and Ellis saw how this eleven-year-old broke down $20.

He said, "Mr. Andre I took $5 got a haircut; I'll take another $5 to take the bus to the roller-skating rink and back; with the other $5 I'm going to pay my way in and rent some skates and with the other $5 I get to get a hotdog and a soda."

The next Saturday, Jermaine showed up to the garden with five other boys. "See, I told you Mr. Ellis was going to give us $20 for skating but we got to work four hours."

The program was born. And while the neighborhood started to change, things don't happen overnight.

In 53206, death is still all too common. Just blocks from the garden are several teddy bear memorials to mark where someone lost their loved one to violence.

Ellis and his meditation soon turn to prayers.

His silent prayers become loud.

"God, I know everything is in your hands. I ask that you please lay your hand on Doobie. Spare him Lord. Amen," he said.

He then bends down to pull a few weeds from the tomato patch. His hands shake as tears begin to roll down his face. His eyes are red and puffy from a lack of sleep.

The last thirty-two hours have sent Ellis on an emotional roller-coaster.

On Saturday, August 11, 2018, fifty-six boys showed up to the garden by 8:00 a.m. to clean up the neighborhood, earn $20 for their work, and talk about how they can be advocates for change.

Ellis's message was clear. "Don't pay attention to what they say about you on the news. You can be better than that. Prove them wrong."

Some of the boys hugged Ellis and told him happy birthday ahead of his Monday celebration. On Sunday, Ellis invited friends, family, and the community to the garden to help him kick off his fifty-eighth birthday. Dozens of people came to eat, socialize, listen to old school music, and thank the man who has been the "earth dad" to many in the neighborhood.

The outdoor celebration allowed Ellis to showcase all the good that comes from the community garden. Residents could feast on cucumbers, zucchini, tomatoes, greens, and green beans in an area that was once void of life. Just barren land. The now flourishing garden has been used as a place of peace.

Neighbors at odds have been brought to the garden by Ellis to settle their disputes before they turned violent, often solving their beef over a burger or brat.

The garden has also become a place where people can come to meditate, read, or just take fresh fruit and vegetables if they need it.

Ellis also used the day to celebrate the boys, who he said gave him a reason and a purpose to live.

"A lot of them in the beginning were coming just for the $20 because I know a lot of them need it, but now I believe they come for the mentorship. They come to the garden because they know they have people here who believe in them and want to see them become successful the right way," Ellis said.

There's Maleak Taylor, fifteen, who was working the grill Sunday.

Maleak was one of about a dozen youth from Milwaukee who were selected to spend ten days in Washington, D.C., to see how our government works. Maleak, who Ellis nicknamed "Lil Obama," used to be a troublemaker at LaFollette Middle School, across the street from the garden, but after working with Ellis for three years, he graduated from the school as the school's salutatorian.

"I always saw great things in Maleak," Ellis said. "He just needed to see it in himself. I refused to let him not be great."

Ellis said he told Maleak that he reminded him of President Obama because of his ears. Three years after giving him that nickname, Maleak sent Ellis a picture from Washington sitting at the desk of the former president.

As Maleak seasoned chicken wings and placed them on the grill, Ellis continued to mentor, showing Maleak just how much seasoning to add and how to know when to flip the chicken over.

"He can't help himself," Maleak said. "But I know he cares. He really do."

Maleak said for a while, he let the anger of his father not being in his life affect him negatively. "I didn't really care about school and I didn't realize it was because I was really mad because my father was not there," Maleak said. "Mr. Andre told me that he may not be my birth dad but he could be my earth dad and he's been there for me ever since."

Maleak said he had a hard time trusting men at first because the men he knew never kept their promises.

"I was waiting for (Mr. Andre) to leave but he never did. He never turned his back on me," he said.

Maleak's father has been incarcerated most of his life, but he said his mother has been one of his biggest supporters. "Mr. Andre" has also been there for Maleak to talk about anything from school to life.

As Sunday's neighborhood celebration came to an end and people started to pack up, Ellis was looking forward to sharing a quiet birthday with his wife on Monday.

But as he locked the gate to the garden at about 8:25 p.m. Sunday, he heard gunshots ring out. They were close and he had a feeling in his gut that something was not right.

"I felt something in my stomach, so I sat down and I told my neighbor that it wasn't good," Ellis said.

Soon, squad cars were rushing down Ninth and Ring to Tenth and Burleigh Street. Ellis got on the phone and started calling the homes of boys who lived in that direction. Call after call was good news. His boys were safe.

Then he got a call from his longtime friend June Thomas, who serves as a mentor in the garden.

"Mr. Andre, Eric is dead and they shot the baby boy, too. The baby so far is alright," Thomas said.

Eric Williams served as an adult mentor in the garden in 2017. He was killed after someone opened fire into a crowd of people. His four-year-old son Doobie was shot four times—twice in the upper chest and once in each arm. Williams was pushing his other son in a stroller at the time of the shooting and witnesses said he used his body as a shield to protect his children.

Ellis said Williams, twenty-eight, took six shots in the back to make sure his children survived. Williams died at the scene, just a block away from where his brother Kevin was killed eight months prior. A teddy bear shrine is tied to a tree where Kevin was shot. Blue, red, and silver balloons line a light pole on Tenth and Burleigh where Eric took his last breath.

Milwaukee police say the shooting stemmed from a long-standing feud. A fourteen-year-old boy who suffered a graze during the incident worked in the garden. The teen said he has been to too many funerals over the past two years to count. He said he was angry and he wanted revenge.

"Eric was a good dude. He didn't mess with anybody. Now I have to step up and help raise his kids," he said. "This is so messed up bro. I really want to get them like they got my cousin. I know nobody wants to hear that, but that's really what I want to do."

Stopping retaliation is something that keeps Ellis up at night. His wife Angela said most people don't see what happens after the children leave the garden.

They don't see how Ellis stops a lot of the violence by getting in the middle of things, she said.

When Williams was shot, Angela said her husband walked down to the scene and calmed down a situation that was getting heated between the police and grieving family members.

Ellis was close to Williams and his son. Ellis pitched in to help bury his brother when he had nowhere else to turn. He also helped Williams when he needed help for the funeral for his mother in 2016.

Williams always expressed how grateful he was and he gave back by helping to mentor the boys in the garden. He did not participate that summer because he was still dealing with the loss of his own brother.

On Monday, August 13, 2018, Ellis's birthday, all he could wish for was Doobie's recovery.

On his social media page, Ellis posted that his prayer was being answered. At 12:38 pm on August 15, 2018, Ellis posted, "Doobie is breathing on his own. They took the tube out and he's trying to talk. Keep praying y'all God is working a miracle right in front of our eyes. We still need to keep praying. Take a moment and shout thank you God!"

Williams's death wasn't the first to touch the garden this year.

The community garden got off to a somber mood when it kicked off on June 16, 2018, and one face was visibly missing but not forgotten.

Dennis "Booman" King, fifteen, was beaten and stabbed to death in May after it was alleged that he took someone's video game system. King worked in the garden and was well known among many of the boys who participated in the program.

There are success stories that come out of 53206 and one showed up on a recent Saturday in the garden.

Muhibb Dyer, who grew up in 53206, is a community activist and nationally-known spoken word artist. He took to a small stage in the garden while holding his daughter, and began to share his story. He had the boys stand up and repeat: "I WILL NOT DIE YOUNG!"

Muhibb told the boys he took a recent vacation with his wife in Miami, Florida, and he was swimming in the ocean and he could look around and see sandy beaches and palm trees.

It looked nothing like where he grew up.

Muhibb grew up on North Twelfth Street and West Ring, just four blocks away from the garden. "I grew up not far from a street called Burleigh that many refer to as 'The Zoo,'" he said.

He went on to talk about some of the young men he grew up with in the neighborhood who were addicted to the street life. He lost many childhood friends to violence and prison just from his block.

One friend got caught with a couple kilos of cocaine and is serving sixty years in prison. One robbed a bank and is now doing twenty-five years and another one was stabbed by his girlfriend and he took the knife out of himself and stabbed her and they both died.

"When you go through that, you must say to yourself, 'How did I get here?'" he said. "A little black boy swimming in the ocean looking at palm trees in a place looking like heaven and I came from a place that look like hell."

Muhibb said the thing that saved him from ending up like his friends is because he remembered that they wanted "hood respect," but he wanted "world respect."

When you want hood respect, you don't give a damn how you make your money. You want to make your money even if you must destroy everything around you. When you want hood respect, you don't care if you shoot up a playground and kids are on it. You don't care whose families you are tearing apart. If you make your money, you are good, Muhibb explained.

When you want world and community respect, you decided for yourself early in life that you are going to build up yourself and everyone around you.

Muhibb put his daughter down and reached into his black backpack and pulled out his college degree and held it high so the boys could see it.

The degree represented more than 1,000 hours of study, and while his friends were having a good time partying, Muhibb said he wanted to be with them as well, but he wanted world respect.

"When you want world respect, you build yourself. You get educated and you decide you are going to make your money giving hope. You are going to make your money giving dreams. You are going to make your money making your hood better than how you received it," he said.

When you want hood respect, the hood loves you but your kids don't.

"You loving the block, you not loving your kids. When you want world respect, you bring your kids with you. That's why I brought my daughter here today because I want her to say, 'My daddy was a great man. My daddy loved me. My daddy was in my life.'"

When Muhibb asked the boys to raise their hands if they grew up without their fathers in their lives nearly all of the fifty-six kids in the garden that day raised their hands.

"Just because you grew up without your father don't mean you can't be better than who your father was," he said.

Muhibb give one last example of hood respect versus world respect.

When you want hood respect you want people to fear you, but when you want world respect, you want people to love you, like Mr. Andre Lee Ellis loves you, he said.

"In the hood, you want a gun to speak for you. In the world, you want your actions to speak for you," Muhibb said. "Mr. Andre don't do this for money. He try to get money for y'all, at the expense of himself. He do this for the pride, the dignity, the respect and honor of being a good man."

About 90 percent of the boys participating in the program come from homes led by a single parent and more than 80 percent of the boys don't have a relationship with their fathers.

Ellis told the boys that he never knew his biological father because he died before he was born, but that didn't stop him from being a good man.

"I want you guys to want world respect," Ellis said. "If you have world respect, you can be the change agents this world needs. You guys can be anything you want to be. We planted the seeds right here, now it's time for you to grow."

A List of Sounds That Can Be Heard In Milwaukee

PAIGE TOWERS

On a clear sky morning on Memorial Day in 2018, I made a list of every sound I could hear from the back porch of my little house in the Riverwest neighborhood of Milwaukee. It included the following sounds: my neighbor's pitbull snoring in the grass, the fading bass music of a car several blocks away, a motorcycle engine backfiring. If I had listened in the early afternoon instead, I maybe would have listed "distant gunshot" right after "the whirr of a hummingbird's wings." This is because, that afternoon in a nearby Riverwest park, a young poet was shot and killed just a few dozen feet away from where children played and hot coals simmered in grills.

The people enjoying their holiday in the park said on the news that they saw the poet—a twenty-one-year-old man named Juan Bernal—stumble through the grass with his hands behind his head, looking toward the sky. In the game of "guns or fireworks," more than one witness said they'd been hoping that the loud pop had been the latter, until they noticed the red stain on his shirt.

He fell down near the street and bled to death.

Since reading a book about noise last summer, I've been making daily lists of sounds. The book's author recommended the activity—it's an exercise for developing more awareness of the aural environment you live in. My lists usually start with the obvious: the garbage truck rumbling through the alleyway, police sirens, cars honking, the wind off Lake Michigan rustling the leaves of my neighbor's tree, two men on the street cussing at each other, a weedwacker, now a lawnmower, now birds chirping.

The more time I sit on my top wooden stair with a pen and journal, the more human-produced background sounds I notice, like the constant whoosh of interstate traffic or the high-pitched ring emitted from a nearby factory. Eventually, I feel overwhelmed by the oppressive nature of it. This was the author's point. America's urban dwellers are living in a modern world of too much sound, but we've become accustomed to all this noise pollution, just as we've become accustomed to the violence and crime.

According to data collected in 2015 by the the FBI Uniform Crime Reporting Program, Milwaukee has the tenth highest murder rate in the country. This means that 24.15 out of 100,000 people were victims of homicide in the span of one year. Roughly 80 percent of those victims were black males. The number of murders lowered slightly in 2017, but this slow decline matters little to families who lose loved ones.

I'll admit, at times I can temporarily forget about Milwaukee's crime statistics, like when I'm running on the trail that follows the line of the Milwaukee River, or relaxing on the patio of a local brewery, enjoying the present moment, sip by sip. Other times, just like my reaction to all this noise, I feel like I'm snowed under, even in the midst of a Wisconsin summer.

It's not right for me to write about Bernal—I know this. He was black; I'm white. He grew up with the noise of Milwaukee; I grew up with the sound of cicadas in the flat fields of Iowa. He worked intensely hard to make his own opportunities; as a member of the white middle class, mine were laid out in front of me.

Here's another bit of truth: I didn't know Bernal. As a local writer, I just knew of him.

Yet, in the vibrant, violent, diverse, beautiful, too-loud city of Milwaukee, I simply wish to write that one noise that shouldn't have been lost from this soundscape is Bernal's voice. Even though he was only a couple of years out of high school, Bernal gave poetry workshops to groups of children and adults around town. He graced mics throughout Milwaukee and recited his work. He rapped. He spoke. He incited snaps and tears and applause. And when local teachers, artists, friends, and family members wrote or talked about Bernal after his death, they all used words like "inspiration," "joy," and "potential."

People say the same thing about Milwaukee: it has potential. If only it could overcome its decades of racism, redlining, oppression, and crime.

From the same book that recommended recording a list of sounds, I learned that the modern world has become so loud that millions of people suffer hearing loss due to all the noise. Researchers in Sweden found that the chronic sound of distant traffic raises the rate of depression. In Japan, researchers reported that you're more likely to experience hypertension, which can lead to heart disease, if you live near a highway. The number of hours of sleep lost to exhaust pipes, honking horns, overhead airplanes, and hissing factories is so massive that its effects are untrackable.

The noise is killing us it seems.

Yet, in response to the question of, "How bad?," the blue-collar, no-collar, fighting-for-life people of Milwaukee may list the wolf at the door well before noting the late-night group of Harleys cruising the streets. In a city of segregated lines, there's a lot more than noise doing the killing.

I visited the spot in Kern Park where Bernal was murdered recently and recorded a list of sounds. The loudest noise was the passing traffic on Humboldt Street, but there was also birdsong, the drowsy buzz of insects, and the laughter of children chasing each other around a thick stand of pines. Yet, when I stood in front of Bernal's makeshift memorial, all I could think about was silence.

"What an incredible loss," I say to other Milwaukee writers when we talk about him, as if that helps, as if that even remotely encompasses what people directly affected by his absence feel.

Once, in a silent chamber at a sound lab in Minneapolis, I heard the rush of my own pulsing blood inside my neck. I wondered if that's what people hear right before death. Years ago, I read in a poem that when you're dying, your senses get stripped back raw. The poet imagined that you can hear everything—a squirrel rustling in the grass, a car's tires screeching two blocks away, the distant hum of a window air conditioning unit. Meaning, all this noise is vivid and decipherable in just one quick moment, right before it stops.

I can only fathom whether or not this is true, but what I have witnessed are the aftershocks of Bernal's death still reverberating around Milwaukee. In a comment made on an online post about the poet's death, a man wrote, "My god, I just heard you read last month." Amongst all the shock and grief and horror, this comment triggered one heartening thought within me: his voice.

It was forever recorded in yet another person's list of sounds.

Hard Time

ELIZABETH HARMATYS PARK

He threw hard time parties
You were to come dressed
as if you were busted, broke

Once a guy came wearing
only a barrel, held up by
two red suspenders over
his bare shoulders

The food was cheap and good
They always passed a hat
to pay for the band

There is one blurry picture
of the whole grinning gang
taken the year when even
the photographer was drunk

He always felt sorry for people
who didn't like parties, dancing,
or free and noisy parish festivals

If he saw someone glum
just sitting out the fun
he'd shake his head, then
with regret in his voice

he'd lean toward you and say
"Who don't wanna dance,
that's their hard time."

From Athens, with Hops: Giannis Takes Milwaukee

JOHN GORMAN

When the Milwaukee Bucks took Giannis Antetokounmpo with the fifteenth pick in the 2013 NBA Draft, nobody in Milwaukee (or anywhere else, for that matter) had much idea who he was or what he could do. He'd never been to America, could barely speak English, and hadn't ever competed above a level equivalent in America to a decent YMCA league or backwater AAU.

What film there was of the Greek teenager actually playing basketball was grainy, low-def, and almost comical in its depiction of his exploits against what appeared to be a bunch of dock workers fresh off an extended smoke break. The highlights were extraordinary, all the same, and pointed to a bright future if everything broke right, the odds of which happening, most had to admit, weren't great. Even in an underwhelming year for college prospects, drafting him was a substantial risk for any team to take. For the Milwaukee Bucks, it was borderline insane.

An afterthought locally and a never-thought nationally, the preceding quarter century (save one outlier season that ended in the conference finals) had seen the hometown team fight tooth-and-nail every year to scratch its way into one of the Eastern Conference's last few playoffs spots, only to serve as cannon fodder once there for the league's more powerful, popular, and exciting teams. It'd been well over a decade since the Bucks had a squad, or really even a player, that mattered to anyone south of Kenosha or west of the county line, and that fifteenth pick in 2013 came on the heels of a particularly dispiriting "playoff run" that saw the Bucks sandblasted out of the postseason tournament with extreme prejudice by LeBron James's defending and future champion Miami Heat.

It would have been one thing if the players on that 2013 Bucks team were beloved in the local community or played a fun brand of ball people enjoyed watching, but the roster consisted almost entirely of unsmiling malcontents, apathetic paycheckers, and sub-replacement-level jobbers. A half-full arena was something to get excited about, and as often as not during home games, dance contests between drunk fans on the Jumbotron drew as much cheering as anything happening on the court. Sellouts were a thing of the distant past in the outmoded-the-day-it-opened Bradley Center, and local news treated Milwaukee's NBA team as a second-class citizen to the NCAA's Wisconsin Badgers and Marquette Golden Eagles. (Still to this day, a not-small contingent of local sports fans would be happy to see the Bucks move so city leaders could put all of their efforts into landing Milwaukee an NHL team.)

Any other player in the 2013 Draft would have made more practical sense for the Milwaukee Bucks than Giannis Antetokounmpo, but practical thinking wasn't a luxury the Bucks' brain trust had at the time. They couldn't afford to draft just any good player. They needed to find a savior.

By the time 2018 rolled around, Giannis Antetokounmpo had developed into a bona fide superstar, a no-doubt top ten NBA player, an international sensation the likes of which Milwaukee hadn't seen since the Pabst Brewing Company won that apocryphal blue ribbon for its signature lager at the 1893 World's Columbian Exposition. Seven-feet tall and shredded with muscles, he possessed a boundless athleticism truly extraordinary for a man his size. It's not just that Giannis was a good basketball player: it's that he was so good, at such a young age, with such size, on such an accelerated developmental timeline, both physically and skills-wise, that it was impossible to gauge how good he might ultimately become.

What happened with Giannis in his third, fourth, and fifth seasons is the reason people hope for the best. For those so inclined, he could be used as proof that God exists. Metaphors abound, Giannis's surprising and world-altering development akin to that of penicillin, say, or his discovery by the Bucks not unlike poor cattle ranchers finding a thick vein of crude beneath the sunburnt clay of the soon-to-be-foreclosed-upon family homestead. He's got the same body parts as you or me, but has orchestrated unfathomable feats of athleticism about which the rest of us can only dream. The explosive capacity in his leg muscles ought to be illegal. People aren't supposed to be capable of the things he can do, but he can do them, and if other players aren't careful, he will do these things on and/or over them, as poor Tim Hardaway, Jr. learned one winter night in early 2018.

Not long after halftime in a game at Madison Square Garden against the New York Knicks, Bucks guard Khris Middleton stole the ball from a Knicks player, ran out on the break, and, seeing Giannis keeping pace to his right, tossed the ball high in the air for the big Greek to slam home. Which

Giannis did, of course he did, with absolute maximum authority on the head of the sole person scrambling back to play defense, Knicks forward Tim Hardaway, Jr. The play happened quickly, and was exhilarating to watch, but in real-time felt like the same-old-same-old transcendence from Giannis that happened several times a game that season, examples of which occurred so frequently that each individual one seemed not worth going crazy over, beyond the usual shout and smile and brief thank you to the universe, lest we burn ourselves out on his excellence or, worse, miss its next display.

But then something else happened. Once the individual shouts, smiles, and hosannas ceased, it was hard not to notice that the people closest to the action—fans seated courtside, assistant coaches, the other players, those both in the game and on the benches—had strange looks on their faces: eyes fixed, mouths open, minds apparently wiped clean, and not by an abiding sense of wonder and thanksgiving so much as abject terror and confusion.

The announcers' tones of voice changed, too, upon seeing replays, their excited yelps dissolving into hushed disbelief. They assumed they'd seen one thing prior to reviewing the play, but then those replays showed something quite different. Where we thought Giannis leaked out on a fast break and dunked a basketball on the head of poor Tim Hardaway, Jr., in actuality seven-foot Giannis Antetokounmpo ran at a full sprint in the middle of a professional basketball game at the sport's most famous arena and jumped directly over the top of all six feet and seven inches of poor Tim Hardaway, Jr.

It was something to see on TV, but the faces of those closest to the action told a completely different story. It was as though everyone in the immediate vicinity was caught wrestling with the aftermath of having seen something they couldn't possibly have seen, because such a thing should not have been possible. Those men and women clearly believed they knew everything they needed to know about life and the nature of reality up to that moment, and Giannis, in one play, soaked those pretty little beliefs and assumptions with gasoline and set them all on fire.

In post-game interviews, a grinning Giannis told reporters that there was no premeditation or intent prior to the play that, months later, would be named the NBA's Dunk of the Year. Giannis said he hadn't made a conscious decision to jump over Tim Hardaway, Jr., because he didn't know that Tim Hardaway, Jr. was standing there in the first place. Focused on getting into proper position for the finish, he kept his eyes on his teammate, and on the ball, and when that ball was served up, he jumped and grabbed it and slammed it through the hoop, same as he'd always done. Until he saw the replay, that was all he knew that happened. This ridiculous moment that broke the space-time continuum, it turned out, was mostly just an accident.

Before anyone called him the Greek Freak, before he saved a moribund franchise from polite midwestern obsolescence, Giannis Antetokounmpo was a skinny kid with a huge smile living very far from home.

The adjustments he had to make as a rookie are startling to think about in hindsight. There might not be two cities on Earth more diametrically-opposed than Giannis's hometown of Athens, Greece, and Milwaukee, Wisconsin. They do not share one single superficial or historical detail or characteristic, save perhaps that both were founded on large bodies of water, though even there, the Mediterranean Sea and Lake Michigan aren't exactly the same thing (they aren't even the same kind of water). One city is thousands of years old, the other less than two hundred, and the local climates and cultures are near-total opposites, Athens sun-splashed and famous for its heart-healthy local diet, Milwaukee frozen half the year and renowned for, well, not having a heart-healthy local diet.

There were also plenty of personal considerations that could have made Giannis's first year in America as much of a nightmare as it was a dream come true. He was nineteen, had never been far from home, didn't speak much English, had neither a driver's license nor a car, and lived his entire life to that point in a two-bedroom home surrounded by his parents and three brothers; upon being picked by the Bucks, he lived in a mid-level city without much Greek influence in a foreign country across an ocean from the rest of his family in an apartment by himself. Now, Giannis wasn't totally alone during his first year, as a variety of agents, handlers, and interpreters were on-hand to help him get comfortable with his new surroundings. The Bucks owner at the time, too, former US Senator Herb Kohl, did everything he could to ease Giannis's transition, including using his governmental knowledge and experience to speed up the immigration process for the rest of the Antetokounmpos. While it did eventually work out, and they joined him in Milwaukee by season's end, Giannis had to go through most of his rookie year on his own, without seeing his family.

Even so, Giannis still wanted to help them make ends meet, and sent money back to Greece as often as he could. One November afternoon early in his first season, a blustery day with a high in the twenties, Giannis took a cab to the Western Union near his apartment on the city's East Side prior to heading to the Bradley Center for that night's game. Exactly how much or how little money Giannis wired that day to his family is unknown, but whatever the total, it amounted to every dime he had on him. A noble gesture, to be sure, but also a stupid one, in that awareness-lacking teenage way, given that he still had to get to the stadium, had planned on taking another cab, and not only was he now out of money, but his credit card wasn't working.

The easiest path to the Bradley Center from that Western Union covers approximately three miles, over Farwell to Brady down Water to downtown and across the river to the arena. Giannis didn't yet own a winter coat or hat, and he'd left the house that day in team-issued sweats unsuited to prolonged exposure to the cold, but that didn't matter. He was out of other options and needed to get to the arena come hell or high water. So, he did what came naturally. He took off running.

Thankfully, someone recognized him as he ran past, which was no small miracle considering the state of the team at the time. This was before the billionaire ownership group and the brand new stadium and attached commercial development, ahead of his face being plastered all over town with the "Own the Future" slogan and prior to his leading the team to consecutive playoff appearances. The team only won fifteen games in his rookie season, and Giannis barely played. He also didn't go to an American college, didn't play in March Madness, and hadn't been a high school phenom. Bucks fans spent most of that season simply learning how to pronounce his name, and yet, a random passing stranger getting into her car after an afternoon shopping with her boyfriend couldn't believe it when she saw Giannis Antetokounmpo running down the Brady Street sidewalk.

"Is that the new kid?" she thought, and upon confirming it was, caught up to him a few blocks down to see if he needed help.

"Are you going to the Bradley Center?" he asked.

Almost certainly not, nobody went near that place until game time, not unless they worked there or at an adjacent business. But seeing him running like that, there could be no response other than "Of course!" and Giannis folded his lanky body into the back of the warm Honda Fit that ferried him the remaining mile-and-change to the arena.

This story would not have taken place in most NBA cities, because unlike Milwaukee, most NBA cities hit one or all of the following criteria: they are home to millions of people well-versed in minding their own business; they have expansive public transit systems or, conversely, punishing urban sprawl; they are in warm weather climates that lower the stakes of being caught outside in November; and they feature large, passionate, engaged local fan bases. Giannis wouldn't have been able to run across town to the arena in Houston or Dallas, couldn't rely on a passing driver's kindness in New York or Los Angeles, wouldn't find it a big deal to be caught outside in November in Miami or San Antonio, wouldn't have trouble hopping a train in Chicago or the Bay Area, and wouldn't go largely unrecognized on a city street in Portland or Boston.

No, this Giannis story is a Milwaukee story, perhaps the most Milwaukee story, and Giannis, without knowing it, acted in the most Milwaukee way possible. An amazing, you might say ludicrous, confluence of circumstances came together so that a green-as-green-can-be teenage basketball prodigy from the other side of the world sprinted across Milwaukee in sweats in twenty-degree weather to play in an NBA game after sending all the money he had on him to his family in Greece, only to be stopped halfway and offered a ride in a kind stranger's hatchback that dropped him off at his NBA arena's service entrance on time and free of charge.

Milwaukee is very much not for everybody, but anyone willing to do what's necessary to get where they need to go won't have too much trouble with the place. From the moment fans heard this story, and it spread like a brush fire once public, whoever this kid ended up being as a player—and remember, nobody had any idea what that might be—we figured we were going to have a pretty good time together. And yes, sure, perhaps Giannis Antetokounmpo would have become a superstar if he played in one of those other NBA cities, but the fact is he didn't become a superstar playing in one of those other NBA cities. He became one playing in Milwaukee.

Shorty

VIANCA ILIANA FUSTER

A version of this story originally ran on 88Nine Radio Milwaukee.

Pa-da-tat, pa-da-tat, pa-da-tat, pa-da-tat. "I could do this all day," Shorty yells to me, over the speed bag. Pa-da-tat, pa-da-tat, pa-da-tat, pa-da-tat.

Israel "Shorty" Acosta has a "living legend" presence to him. He rhythmically hits the speed bag while staring at me with the the most genuine smile I've ever seen. Pa-da-tat, pa-da-tat, pa-da. He missed the speed bag that time, giggled, and invited me into his office in the United Community Center (UCC).

One wall in his office is covered with photos and old news articles. His most recent successes are documented next to a photo of a young Shorty with professional boxer Muhammad Ali. Another wall with hooks holds a rainbow of lanyards from different boxing competitions around the world.

His priority is to show me a photo of him and one of his winning boxers, despite having an intimate photo with the world's greatest boxer of all time. He never mentions it, but humbly tells the story of the photo with the People's Champ when visitors inevitably ask.

Shorty is a man with a lot of stories. He's a walking anthology of knowledge about the competitive boxing circuit in the Midwest, as well as at the Olympic and professional level. Despite the amount of successful boxers to come through his South Side gym, being humble is just who Shorty is.

"I don't know, I think it's something that God gave to me," said Shorty.

He began his boxing career after moving to Milwaukee from Puerto Rico in 1973. In his words, his brother gave him no time to "bum around." The first thing he did was take Shorty to the original UCC boxing gym on Sixteenth Street.

"See, when we came in 1973 to Milwaukee, my brother Daniel said, 'You're not going no place, you're going with me to the gym.' And I started fighting, and everybody said, 'You fought before.' No, never."

Gym rats and coaches around him became instantly aware of his natural ability. Many of them thought he'd been boxing for years, even though it had just been months. "I used to get out of the South Division pool and jump into the gym, that used to be my life," said Shorty.

After competing in the Golden Gloves—a national amateur boxing tournament—he began to compete nationally, internationally, and almost went to the Olympics.

Shorty would have his first shot at becoming an Olympic medalist in 1980, but fell short when his team never made it to the games. That year, President Jimmy Carter was boycotting the competition as it was being held in what was formerly known as the Soviet Union. No Olympians were sent on behalf of the US team that year.

Shorty would go on to try again in 1984. He moved on from the first round and lost to Paul Gonzalez by split decision. He boxed for another ten years until his retirement in 1994 to become a full-time boxing coach.

"I fought 500 times. Fighting international I got forty-three international competitions. I used to be fighting and coaching at the same time," said Shorty. "Not too many people do that."

"I remember when I used to be a little kid I used to say, 'I want to go to Australia.' And my dream came true when I went to coach the Olympic team. I don't show my Olympic rings, I left them at home. I got three Olympic rings, you know, not too many people got that."

His time as a coach would prove to be just as successful as his boxing career. Shorty trained several young boxers into professional competitors with names like Luis Feliciano, Luis Cuba Arias, and Javier Martinez on his short list of winning fighters. Shorty's three Olympic rings come from his time coaching the Australian and London Olympic games in 2000 and 2012.

Shorty said: "To go international, you have to be 100 percent in shape. That's what I told Javielito"—Javier "Javielito" Martinez, his current boxing prodigy—"He gotta be fighting, you know. Don't take a break."

Martinez was born and raised on the South Side of Milwaukee. He began training with Shorty at age eight. "He's like a father to me," said Martinez. "I feel comfortable with him. We have a lot of chemistry."

Martinez is now twenty-two and competes as an amateur. He's working with Shorty toward a professional career and a spot on the 2020 Olympic boxing team.

"I've been a national champion about four times, won state about six or eight times, and it's tough," said Martinez. "People think it's just coming in here and punching something—it's not. It's a lot to it. Losing weight— it's stressful. Them nerves before a fight, not a lot of people can handle it. It's tough—getting punched in the face is not for everybody."

Shorty, the former Olympic hopeful turned Olympic champion coach, reflected on Martinez and himself.

"He's going to compete now. The same way that I used to do, now he do it—you know, that's what makes me proud," said Shorty. "I think we're the best in the Midwest no matter what, you know. And we're growing more and more."

Shorty and his wife, Dora Acosta, have been longtime educators at UCC, the South Side beacon that includes schools, senior centers, performance centers, art galleries, a restaurant, and the boxing gym. Their commitment and dedication to the school led to the new Acosta Middle School being named in honor of their service to the South Side community. While his wife retired a few years ago, Shorty imagines he'll still be making his way to his boxing gym.

"Will you ever retire?" I asked. He smiled and said, "Maybe when I'm in a wheelchair . . . I'm still here," he said, indicating a wheelchair wouldn't be enough to keep him away.

"To be here, to teach the kids, to keep the kids out of trouble—and I'm still here. I don't know, maybe I'll be here for a while."

It's hard not to freak out over a man who has photos with Evander Holyfield, Mike Tyson, and the great Muhammad Ali, but he shows them off with humility and pride. No matter the amount of trophies, no matter the number of successful boxers and accomplishments, Shorty says he's just "the same ol' Shorty."

When you step into the ring with Shorty, you step into his home and his heart. He eagerly welcomes you in and is anxious to teach you how to hit the speed bag.

The Heartbeat of a World

HARVEY TAYLOR

Chuck is led into the room by someone's arm,
then his hand is guided to a chair.
I tell him I'm glad he's here for music class;
he replies, "OK."
As he's given instruments, he plays methodically,
a scientist of sound, a connoisseur of vibrations,
investigating subtleties that others may not perceive;
a triangle, for example, might tingle the skin of someone
for whom careful listening is a matter of survival.

After our weekly session of acoustic experiments,
I take Chuck out to the hallway, where he feels
for the wall he'll follow to the dining room,
moving his hands along a beautiful mural depicting Milwaukee,
with people portrayed in front of the Center For Independence,
some in wheelchairs, some with canes, some with sunglasses on:
he passes by them all, and those watching from skyscraper windows,
and others walking into the Mitchell Park Domes, and
children on a see-saw, and birds flying in-between clouds—
Chuck keeps going, around the corner of the corridor,
past the zoo, to the lakefront, where seagulls soar, and
sailboats catch the wind, and a volleyball floats permanently
in the blue sky, and . . . right where kids are making sandcastles,
just beyond the splashing waves, Chuck stops, and
stands before the painting he can't see,
except with his fingertips . . . and begins hitting the wall
with the heel of his left hand, Boom,
then raps twice with his right-hand knuckles, da-da,
          Boom da-da, Boom da-da,
the rhythm inherited from his mother's heartbeat,
          Boom da-da, Boom da-da,
primal music, surging from deep within,
          Boom da-da, Boom da-da,
bare hands on a painted drum: the heartbeat of a world

"Art is Collaboration": Xavier Leplae and Riverwest Radio

ZACK PIEPER

Every city contains its nexus of unique neighborhoods; and within each neighborhood continually emerges its cast of defining characters—not "mascots" per se—but personifications of some specific trait, some niche interest, all speaking divergently; but to and from the same spirit of that particular locale. These are the shop owners and artists, barkeeps and collectors, organizers and regulars, who will nab any chance to register their civic outrage, extrapolate upon shared cosmologies, or to verbalize their speculations and daydreams. In short, talkers.

In Milwaukee, there exists no more of a complete and representative roll call of such voices than Riverwest Radio—an entirely community-run and operated FM radio station, situated in the storefront of an archaic film and video rental shop, Riverwest Film and Video. The programming isn't just a vehicle for a host of diverse concerns—social, political, aesthetic— it's also a living portrait, in sound, of a neighborhood in itself. Few other cultural hubs more perfectly define this neighborhood's particular penchant for collaborative, out-in-the-open dialogue, and off-the-cuff creation. Perhaps small, relatively cheap cities make themselves most amenable to the cross-pollination of different art scenes, to intimacy and collaboration. Why shouldn't most of your audience also be your potential or active collaborators? How could they not be?

Milwaukee's Riverwest neighborhood has long been an area close enough in proximity to one of the city's major economic fault lines to still ensure (for now) fairly cheap rents; as fly-by-night galleries and DIY art spaces have arrived and disappeared with relative frequency for several decades. And while Riverwest Radio has become a proper, nonprofit entity, it is also one in a long line of communal art-making, and non-institutional, performance spaces, scattered throughout Milwaukee in the nineties to the mid-aughts.

One of these touchstones, who has frequented, instigated, and facilitated many such spaces, is Riverwest Film and Video's proprietor, and

Riverwest Radio's founder and station director, Xavier Leplae. Or, as most Milwaukeeans know him: Xav.

Xav has always been involved in Riverwest and in organizing creative venues. Some of these precursory spaces include his Junk Cheap shop, which blurred the line between a store, an art studio, and an anything-goes performance space (while also offering for sale an assortment of interesting junk). In the early nineties, the shop expanded into a homemade TV studio and pirate radio station called Sugar Free Radio, which led to the house-front micro-radio station Wireless Virus. A few years later, he was a primary collaborator with director Chris Smith and others on Milwaukee's *Zero TV*, an early, groundbreaking, pre-YouTube internet channel; and in the early 2000s, he ran a gallery, performance space, and pumpkin store called Pumpkin World. Throughout these, he operated Chez Xav, a back of the store, pay-what-you-can-afford restaurant; and co-created Soup and Cinema, a film screening series with poet and moviemaker Stephanie Barber in her Bamboo Theater. After her departure from Milwaukee, Xav also helped run playwright and performer Theresa Columbus's legendary Darling Hall theater, performance, and party space.

All these spaces and projects situate Riverwest Radio as a concept not far from Xav's tendency toward the collaborative and the socially-immersive.

"My strong suit really is collaboration . . .," he says, "I guess I've always primarily been a person who thrives in an environment of more communal ways of making things . . ."

While initially a streaming internet station situated in the storefront of Xav's film supply and DVD rental business, Riverwest Radio and its roster of hosts, volunteers, and conversationalists, has come to generate most of the video store's constant (and sometimes atonal) buzz of hive-like activity.

And a very buzzing hive it is. Entering the shop, through the plastic flower-laden screen door (Xav also has a penchant for dimestore mosaics and Bollywood kitsch), one passes through a flurry of activity.

"Welcome Toooo Theeee Neeeiiighhbooorrrhooooddd," intones rhapsodizing monologist C. C. Carmichael, in a black Stetson hat in one shop window to a recorded background of endangered birds chirping. His show is something of a mix between spoken word poetry, folk wisdom, and daily affirmations. A mother and son browse the DVD collection (Xav continues to offer DVDs for rental, both rare and new) as two apprehensive students in flip-flops trickle in to buy filmstock. A postal carrier drops off a box of vintage *Playboy* magazines. Me: "Who the hell are these for?" Xav: "I order them off eBay for this one guy who comes in here . . ." A young woman is painting sparkles on the end of a stick, sitting under a large shelf of low-tech consoles. A wiry flower vendor and local fixture known as "Rabbi" (a frequent guest and briefly host of his own show, "Spider Mike and The Rabbi Tell Jokes") insists everyone within earshot try a "still good" elderflower and club soda beverage he's recently recovered in a dumpster dive. "Still good . . . still good . . . see?" In the cooking/meeting/hangout space behind the register is Xav, calm but not melancholy, in his early fifties, wearing one of his trademark knit beanies, large gold glasses, and a bright yellow sweater emblazoned with a white felt poodle. He keeps attempting to resume a small meeting about fundraising, to email local business sponsors, all while simultaneously searching for a Band-Aid for Rabbi. The atmosphere is more *Cannery Row* than "Prairie Home Companion."

When Riverwest Radio started in 2011, it was two MacBooks, two mixing boards, and a set of relatively inexpensive microphones set up in the two large storefront windows of Xav's shop—more of a continuous "sound installation" streamed over the internet than a clearly structured radio station. A diverse succession of talkers, vendors, buskers, hucksters, artists, poets, punks, hippies, historians, daycare workers, teachers, mothers, advocates, activists, playwrights, ex-prisoners, ex-patients, advice-columnists, tarot-readers, movie buffs, impressionists, specialty collectors, journalists, teenagers, misfits, sports fans, union organizers, armchair philosophers, anarchist agitators, homeless veterans, feminists, bakers, eccentrics, ("and don't forget to add: a few con artists," Xav interjects)— comprised the constant stream of voices, all day long, all fixtures from the neighborhood or its surrounding areas, each one after the other, devotedly planting themselves in either of the shop's windows for their hour-long programs; sometimes improvising with passing oglers, sometimes bantering with callers, or just talking to see what they'll say.

In this earlier, more rough-hewn incarnation, literally anyone in the community could (and did) produce any kind of show they wanted, barring the use of obviously copywritten music or harmful language. Weekly time slots were allotted, and shows were created and cancelled with regularity. Some early programs created by neighborhood regulars included "Smoke With Your Boy: Sleepy G and Friends"; "Uncle Al Matzoball"; "Hakobo's Hodgepodge"; "Hussle Responsibly"; "Children's Stories with JoAnn Chang"; "Ingrid's Inspirational Hour"; and "Jim and Friends Read the News"; among numerous others regretfully omitted here.

From 2011 to 2013, the shop also became a kind of testing ground or laboratory for live radio experiments of all kinds, often instigated by artists of varying disciplines and mediums. Examples such as "Ching Suru" (improvised sound/noise collages by visual artists Chuck Quarino and Santiago Cuculla) and "Hello Caller" (a conceptual call-in show created by Xav and myself) explored narrative threads in manipulated sound, and often wacky, elaborate call-in experiments. "Subtle Forces" (from artists/performers Anja Notanja Sieger and Freesia McKee) also investigated the strangeness of daily minutiae through various improvised radio-specific scenarios.

There were shows entirely comprised of shout-outs, marathon readings of books, musical improvisation, play-by-plays of mundane events, coverage of the local twenty-four-hour bike race, ringtone symphonies, fake product reviews, prank calls, and extended conversations (sometimes hours-long, and sometimes with a passerby) at all hours of the night.

Besides being a facilitator for dialogue and experimentation, Xav has also variously been lauded (though quietly) for his work in film, performance and installation art, as well as video and sound art. He's acted in dozens of films by peers in the film and video community (see *Chaza Show Choir* and *Hamlet 2020AD*) and been a member of countless bands and performance groups (XKS, The Album Bums, etc.). He still creates temporary art spaces, formulates unique events, and each year improvises sets of video mashups projected on a massive screen for Milwaukee's annual New Year's dance party, The Get Down.

There is no doubt the term multidisciplinary would most easily apply to Xavier's output over the years, as it would for many of his past and present Milwaukee peers. Yet in his practice there's always been this tendency toward blurring the line between passive documentation and active participation. Between the created and the found.

"As a kid, I went through a long period where I documented everything. Like, almost everything that happened to me or my friends or family . . . Everyone is an archivist these days, by default. But I always wanted to play with whatever it means to record or capture something, to retell it, or displace it somehow . . ."

Xav comes from a family of artists, travelers, and first-generation immigrants. He grew up to the gentle and continuous patter of conversation in his family's modestly-sized home in the Shorewood neighborhood just north of Milwaukee's city limits. With five siblings, communal modes of creation were undoubtedly ingrained. Xav's father, Luc Leplae, was a physics professor, an intellectual, and an artist, born in Belgium, where he studied under esteemed physicist Ilya Prigogine. Xav's grandfather was the well-known Belgian sculptor Charles Leplae. To this day, his father's youthful physique remains the model for the figure that adorns the logo on bottles of Stolichnaya vodka. Luc met Xav's mother Genevieve on the Queen Mary, en route from France, himself heading toward a Ph.D. in Maryland. After years of teaching physics at UW-Milwaukee, he turned his focus to creating autobiographical comic books, depicting his pre-pubescence in Belgium during the German Occupation, and detailing his hallucinatory and ecstatic experiences after receiving a liver transplant, including the belief that he was sharing his body with the soul of an African American mother. Luc, Genevieve, and their family traveled widely. Perhaps something in their outlook was uniquely post-war European; pragmatic but not moralistic, thrifty but effusive, open to the world in the way only an outsider can be.

After Shorewood High graduation, a brief stint at Cooper Union art school, and following an impulsive (and by his account "largely capricious") move to join, then abandon, the Army Reserves in 1985, Xav returned to his family and friends to attend UW-Milwaukee's burgeoning film and media department. He studied with filmmakers Kathy Cooke and Rob Danielson just before the department began to welcome such notable experimental film luminaries as George Kuchar and Robert Nelson.

During this period Xav recognized his own temperament's most amenable mode: dialectical and collaborative, with a penchant for experimental live transmissions. Following the lead of the film department, and a nationwide trend in state-funded local programming in the early eighties, he ensconced himself in creating content for Milwaukee Public Access TV with friends including Martin Hallanger, who after many years of working corporate at Kmart has reunited with Xav to become Riverwest Radio's program director. Says Hallanger: "In the public access days, we did a lot of really nutty stuff: odd games, audience response, viewer collaboration. We once had a figure drawing class with a live model, so asked viewers to send in their drawings, and one by one, superimposed them over our live models. That was amazing. The models had to stay still for a long time! . . . We had lots of clear and defined concepts, but asked viewers to write in, to determine its content, whatever course that took."

In 1988, Xav's growing interest in film and videomaking led him to China, accompanying his father Luc, who was then teaching and receiving his masters at Yunnan University in Kunming. There, Xav interned under director Yu Xiao Yang, a sort of *enfant terrible*, enamored with New Wave cinema, the son of a famous actor, and a spoiled brat who would regularly throw tantrums on the set.

One day in 1989, he met the director by chance, as a crowd grew to unexpected proportions in Tiananmen Square. "I remember clearly hearing bullets zip past just before I bumped into him. First, the park almost felt like this huge stage. There was this sense of almost exhilaration, of witnessing history . . . Then slow waves of panic, it wasn't like a stage anymore." Xav was directed to the Belgian embassy and departed within the week.

Settling immediately in New York, he worked as a cab driver, attempted a storefront video studio, and organized Planet Bushwick, a dada-esque video art collective. His earlier inspiration from Public Access and broadcasting led him to Paper Tiger, a nonprofit collective made up of volunteers, producing weekly public access television programming that critiqued corporate media, culture, and politics. Founded in 1981, the station grew out of New York's Public Access, and keenly informed Xav's interest in broadcast media as an interface for subversion, social critique, and broader activism.

After returning to Milwaukee for a few years, Xav set off again in 1996, this time with his brother Didier and a crew of fellow filmmakers and artists (Peter Barrickman, Kiki Anderson, Kirsten Stoltmann, Brent Goodsell, and Doug Schall) to film *The Foreigners*—a fantasia entirely filmed in Goreme, a small town in Turkey. The majority of the feature-length film was improvised, concerning the exploits of a hapless space photographer as he wanders off a photoshoot, encountering various inhabitants, and exploring the town's "lunar landscapes." As Didier relates, "When the film was threatened to be shut down by the town's mayor, we all decided the best course of action would be to give him a role in the movie. He was okay with us then. No problems." Indeed, a hilarious and transcendent highlight of the film is a tour of this "moon village" conducted by the mayor of Goreme himself.

Xav's several trips to India culminated in, arguably, his most stunning achievement in film: 2004's *I'm Bobby*—a shot-for-shot remake of the 1973 Bollywood classic, *Bobby*, filmed in Goa and Bombay, featuring a cast of Karnataka street children, and set to the original movie's exact soundtrack. *I'm Bobby* is rapturous in its moments of sublime incongruity. Vankatesh and other migrant child workers (whom Xav befriended and retains strong friendships with to this day) glow with youthful bravura. The romantic and gaudy score is given unexpected resonance as the children alternately mock and passionately inhabit their assigned roles in this playful retelling of the classic Indian melodrama.

He continued to followed up this aesthetic of interpretive adaption into his collaborations *Mary Worth* (a frame-by-frame short adaption of the popular forties comic strip, executed by some of Milwaukee's most distinctive filmmakers in the late nineties) and again, some years later, in *Razor's Edge* (2009), a film based on collaborator Stephanie Barbers's scattered memory of the plot of Somerset Maugham's novel, set against the urban decay and industrial vacuity of twilight Baltimore. In this experimental narrative also, the natural environment, the neighborhood's inhabitants, and the nuances of the location all gradually become recognizable as the silent narrators of the harrowing tale.

One can easily place Riverwest Radio as an extension of these earlier collaborative and locale-specific approaches to filmmaking, documentation, and art creation in general, that characterize Xavier's entire career.

Xav continues to regularly participate in numerous programs, including "The Barbouille Hymn" with his brother, musician and composer Didier, who runs and operates a recording studio in the basement of Riverwest Film and Video. A playful eclecticism is the hallmark: songs, skits, and sound collages. In addition, he has helped create "My Dinner with Gabe" and regularly guests on "Cinema Fireside" (with *Coven* director and writer Mark Borchardt and film buff Gabe Van Handel). Both programs discuss and critique classic, underground, and contemporary movies.

"I mean technically it's a business I'm running, and it's a business that's hosting a radio station, but it would be remiss to say it hasn't functioned as so much more than that . . ."

Since obtaining an FCC license in 2016, through years of art auctions, fundraisers, and a narrow pool of nonprofit grant-writing, Riverwest Radio has remained centered on talk, dialogue, and all variety of unclassifiable transmission. The topics of the programming have also become a microcosm of local concerns and interests; the emphasis has shifted toward activism, rights advocacy, and community engagement.

There is "Ability MKE," advocacy and education from the disabled community, "Youth Rising Up," a platform for urban youth and cultural development, and "Expo: Ex-prisoners Organizing" focuses on social justice and prison reform. Two attorneys host "Legal Briefs," which includes discussions of complex legal issues, statutes, and rulings, two State Represenatives have a show called "State Reppin,'" and city Alderman Nik Kovac's show, "The Packerverse," blends detailed Green Bay Packers post-game commentary with local history, trivia, and robust debate.

There are new programs about Wisconsin wildlife conservation and biology, shows for model railroad enthusiasts and retro video game reviewers. There's "Onion Breath: Radio Theater" and "Sukey's Diner," a cooking show. "In The Field" offers selections of various ambient field recordings, while "Butterfly Mind" digs deep into private press records and oddball recordings. The station's wild eclecticism can be found nowhere else in the neighborhood, and few other places in the city.

Today, at Riverwest Radio, there are still no sound booths, no engineer sitting behind the mixer. The shows still take place in front of the shop's two large storefront windows, providing a uniquely transparent studio, where passersby occasionally stop and listen to the speakers mounted in front of the public bench outside, reinforcing the degree to which the station's participants (who are both hosts and producers) are still looking out at where they live. It is as close to a complete portrait of a diverse locale as could be attempted.

For those Rust Belt towns, or flyover cities, afflicted with inferiority complexes, with complaints of "scene vitality" surrounding the arts and dialogue, who see DIY as more of a style than an ethos, Xav's spirit of letting the atmosphere do the talking is the antidote. Find the Xav in your city, find the people who can never wait to tell you everything necessary and unnecessary, and hit "record." Or just call Xav at (414) 533-5159. Serious. He'll find a place to play your message somewhere.

Milwaukee's Pacific Heritage

CHING-IN CHEN

A version of this work originally ran on the Best American Poetry *blog.*

I write to you from Milwaukee, midwest city, most segregated city in the United States. What it means to write and be in conversation with Asian Pacific Islander American poetry here (a mutated broken-city text, a choral rendering of the many iterations of bodies within this space) feels very different from the Southern California desert where I lived right before moving here or the Massachusetts where I grew up.

[Notes to self, locations to map:
Grand Avenue: Lee Chung's where Wah Lee had complained of theft in fall of 1885, police detectives found little white girl hiding underneath bed]

These last few months in Milwaukee, I have been making poems about the 1889 anti-Chinese riots in Milwaukee. Admittedly, I was looking for traces of this community beyond the Pacific Produce Market or the American Chinese restaurants scattered throughout the city. There is a correlation between this singular event and x's on the map all along the West coast.

[Third Street: Chen Quen where the laundryman at 203 Third Street had two names, Superintendent Whitehead scouring Business District for Chinese laundries and saw at residence and business an adult white woman who was wife of "Jim Young"]

The global body of coolie follows me. Wherever I go, I look for evidences and I try to write about this body. A body next to, laid down beside, amongst, tied to other flesh. A body which points to the ambitions, needs, limits of United States empire. Whatever I write must be relational, must investigate and teach itself the histories and stories and traditions and struggles of other peoples and communities. This is not one body. This body does not exist without other bodies. In-between motion, in-between oceans, in-between mountain blasts, in-between body and body. If I a body of artifact, if I a body of future, if I redevelop cartilage, bone, will you excavate.

[Fifth Street: Hah Ding's laundry where Clara Kitzkow and other girls "visited"]

The evidences regarding an episode of Milwaukee's "forgotten" history, the 1889 anti-Chinese riots. Two middle-aged Chinese men – Hah Ding and Sim Yip Ya – arrested for allegedly taking sexual liberties with white and underaged women. In the census, in the Milwaukee city directory, I ethnically profile by name. I cannot find any like-minded photographs.

[Fourth Street: Ring Shane's laundry (@ State) where windows smashed + Sam Yip Ya's laundry where Clara Kitzkow and other girls "visited"]

Today, at a racial justice gathering for people of color to work through internalized racism, I was startled to see three other APIAs present and to find myself inadvertently in an APIA caucus during a breakout group. The color we are assigned doesn't even register on Milwaukee's segregation map. At lunch, I ask the others who grew up here what it was like. Tightknit or singular.

[Chestnut Street: Joseph Caspari's saloon where effigy of lynched figures + 618 Chestnut where men smashed windows of Chinese laundry @ 1:00 pm >> two Chinese escaped up Winnebago Street]

In her influential essay, "Notes for an Oppositional Poetics," Erica Hunt outlines the projects of dominant languages, wedded to common sense, which serve to anesthetize us, contain us, and encode that containment within our bodies. The struggle and challenge of writing which reconstructs "our recovered histories . . . filled with tales of the wounded," histories which, according to Hunt, "have been omitted, replaced and substituted." And yet to investigate history, to difficult attempt history, to reconstruct history, to re-configure, to struggling with/against the "nostalgia for a lost culture or a sense of unity."

[Jefferson where laundryman described how didn't dare to leave laundry during worst of riot (@ Huron)]

What I don't want to forget: despite { }, there is pleasure here. The body is evidence.

Don't Lose Yourself

FEFE JABER

Once speech season started, Saturdays were all I looked forward to. Waking up at 5:00 in the morning on the weekend with my group of Milwaukee peers to compete against dozens of other Wisconsin high schools, trying to be the funniest person in the room, with the possibility of a first-place trophy . . . I mean what's not to like?

By my senior year, with family seemingly crumbling around me and uncertainty ahead, speech on Saturdays had become my safe haven.

I developed a routine on those early speech competition Saturdays. First, I'd blast "Lose Yourself" by Eminem to help put my "face" on. Get ready for the morning, the sun not usually up yet. Button up my suit, and then get dropped off at my school where the "speech bus" waited for us. Our bus rides consisted of freestyle raps, where everyone took their turns to say how they were going to go home with that first-place trophy. And we all knew, but didn't always say, that this was our time to shine and show the judges, the students, the people from other parts of the state, what us Milwaukee kids were all about.

You knew the Milwaukee kids were in the room as soon as we'd step into the school we were competing at for the day. Whether it was our loud laughter or our bold suits, you knew it was us from afar. We were diverse and quite rowdy, filled with passion for the sport we desperately loved. Don't get me wrong, all the students from the suburban schools enjoyed the activity just as much, but they didn't make an entrance quite like we did. They had a tendency to keep to themselves and practice individually before rounds started. Though they did wish their teammates luck before rounds, it was discreet. For us city kids, we would shout "Kill 'em!" down those hallways. We would practice with one another while giving each other feedback. Most of all, we wore the passion on our faces. A busload of big-city teens, early in morning on a weekend . . . No coffee needed, it was that kind of energy with our group.

For speech competitions, there were many categories—poetry, humorous interpretation, prose, a duo performance—each with its own sets of rules, of which we knew the ins and outs. The variety of categories meant our group of Milwaukee kids didn't usually compete against each other. But even when we did, at smaller speech tournaments, the support was non-stop.

In order to make it through the three preliminary rounds to the final, you needed to meet certain rankings throughout the day. Kellen, one of my teammates, would bring a speaker to every tournament, and as we waited for the rankings to get posted, he'd always blast the same beat, which got our whole group back freestyling. As those postings for the finals were about to go up, we'd stand on the tables, hug one another, and pray that each one of us would see our personal speech "codes" on those large pieces of paper.

Making it to that last round meant you were in the top six of your category, and being able to compete in that final round gave our Milwaukee team the chance to go home with that first-place trophy. No matter whose codes ended up being displayed on those large pieces of paper, the cheering, laughter, and energy would continue. "I didn't make it because I wanted to watch you win that first place."

Every time I advanced to finals, I'd look into the audience and the first people I'd see were my smiling teammates yelling, "Fefe, show them what it means to be funny, kill 'em!" The phrases we'd use to encourage one another may have sounded outrageous to those around us, but let me tell you, we always did "kill 'em." "Those city kids," was a saying that you heard quite often from our opponents.

I am that city kid. I was born into a big Palestinian family in Milwaukee, with an emphasis on big: mom, dad, my three younger sisters and five younger brothers. Even with my family being from a different country, I have always felt normal. Between home, school, and speech competition, my quirks felt as if they matched those of the kids around me. I never thought of myself as being "different" until my first speech tournament. Looking around me, I noticed something unusual. I, for one, was the minority in that room. In Milwaukee, the only world I really knew, I didn't think twice about my Mexican friend Laura or my African American friend Bri. Our cultures were so different, yet we could relate to each other. Milwaukee gave me diversity, pride, and a language. It gave me a new way to communicate and express certain feelings. Milwaukee, quite literally, gave me speech.

And Milwaukee gave me family, of course, though that changed, on March 1, 2013, to be exact. I woke up to a normal school weekday and in the afternoon, I walked home and ran into the kitchen to see what my mom was cooking for dinner. Every time I came home from school, I could smell my mom's home-cooked meals from right outside the front door. Whether it was those freshly stuffed grape leaves or a pot of rice and beans, it was what I looked forward to coming home to after a long day of school.

On this late winter day, not only did I not smell any food, but my mom wasn't in her usual spot in the kitchen. I looked around the house for her and that's when I saw my Dad sitting quietly in the living room. "I'm sorry, but your mom and I will be getting a divorce." I didn't know how to react; I nodded and went into my room to help my siblings with their homework.

My parents' divorce was a nasty one, really taking a toll on me. We moved around a lot and money was extremely tight. There were times when I'd come home from school and there was no one there. There was no one there to talk to or no help in sight. That year was hands down one of the toughest years of my life. I had to grow on my own. I became very independent, trying to give my younger siblings the attention they needed. Taking care of things at home became a priority, making it tough to really do anything else. For food, I got my own dinners; I had never eaten so much fast food.

Speech became my refuge. It wasn't only the activity itself, but the people surrounding me that kept my head up. When Saturdays came along, those bus rides were a reminder that there was still something to look forward to. I looked forward to those rides where I knew I could be myself with the people who mattered most. I looked forward to the raps we made together. My final year in speech, we took home the gold. First place in the whole state of Wisconsin. My team truly did "kill 'em."

Into my senior year, friends all around me had started to receive acceptance letters from their dream colleges. I waited until January for my own miracle letter. When I opened that email from DePaul University that started with "Congratulations," I immediately cried tears of joy. (Well, it was more of an ugly cry but I guess that's what happens when you're genuinely in shock.) I knew from that moment that I would be committing to DePaul and moving to Chicago, which meant I'd be saying goodbye to the people I loved and knew most. It was a hard time still for myself and my family and I wasn't sure I was ready to leave. My heart, though, longed for the new adventures and different perspectives that it takes to make a difference in this world.

It has been more than two years since I've left Milwaukee. Most of my family has moved, too, off to Michigan for their own new adventures (and still close enough to me).

Milwaukee hasn't seen the last of me. As I get closer to finishing my undergraduate degree, I am determined to give back to the city that showed me what I'm truly passionate about. The city that inspired me to continue my education in an even bigger one. The people I grew up with who contributed to my determination to become a politician, to bring a voice to people who feel as if they don't have one. Back to Milwaukee, in time, to the city that showed me diversity, to the city that has given me hardships. To the city that has shared its struggles, strength and love. A "thank you" to the city that has given me inspiration, to the city that has given me motivation.

Blasting Eminem's "Lose Yourself" is still part of my morning routine. The song, believe it or not, makes me smile every time. I don't know if I do it out of habit or if it's because I miss pretending that my rap skills are great. What I do know is, the song reminds me that I won't ever lose anything that Milwaukee has given me.

Notes from the Seasons

MARK BORCHARDT

The pen hits the page in the wondrous magic of autumn, the lush density of summer, the frigid throes of winter, and the beckoning revival of spring. The mysteries that we navigate within Milwaukee are experienced through the tapestries of these four full seasons. Those seasons are immensely appreciated and indulged for all their majestic texture; a rich tetralogy of earthly divergence conjuring a robust alchemy of weather and psychology to accommodate our lives of reading, writing, and thinking critically.

Each season in this city of wonder brings forth a particular tract of instinct. Our spirits enliven with the burgeoning freshness of spring, offering the gateway to summer. Autumn is magical in its untold fury of color, a spectacular display before the heavy oppression of winter formidably descends and conquers the land. Yet, the ethereal fluorescent glow of gas stations veiled in snowy blue twilight in Milwaukee can be as breathtaking as a river running free in the warmer months.

And for some, it is in that abundance of density within each season that they find their true hearts, their sharper intuitions, and examine the deeper recesses of interiority, the complexities of the yearning self, that greater awareness that befits the ceaseless search of larger destinies.

Throughout this seasonal succession of both challenge and enjoyment, Milwaukee provides for a rich coffee shop culture. Each venue provides its own singular environment, its own unique embrace, from the contours of the architecture to the vibrant ebb and flow of its inhabitants. In these establishments I've had some very inspired, enchanting times reading invigorating plays and screenplays. It's also where I've pieced together my own work for theater and film. And I've also enjoyed the companionship of numerous friends and colleagues in the interstices of that work.

And at these coffee shops you encounter the lives of others: brief skirmishes with different worlds. By stepping out of one's door and into the vitality of the general population, the anxiety of solitude can be instantaneously eradicated, for you are immediately informed that you are not alone in the universe. But once there, one cannot afford surrendering the time nor the energy for idle conversations or foolish ideas by others not aligned in the greater glories of one's singular pursuits.

One has to walk the fine line between socialization and greater intent. You must remain firmly fixed in the lands of your own dreams and avoid getting mercilessly caught up in the weary storms of others' ambitions, illusions, and discontents. Work is done in coffee shops to be among the people but not of them, not to the degree that it will impede the attainment of the greater dream of our own theater.

Consequently, in playwriting, the transmutation from the experienced life to its reconfiguration into narrative premise actualizes one's existence into a cathartic alternate reality. It's how we reflect upon, meaningfully interpret, and subsequently present our extemporaneous lives into a dramatic articulation of managed narrative form.

In their more worthy incarnations, it is not through a continuous flow of regimented story-making that these narratives are created; rather, it is an arbitrary receivership of fragmented, intermittent missives from the tenuous borderlands of willed thinking and the subconscious drift that manifests these creative configurations. And it is through honed craft and resilient determination that an ultimate congruency of form is made whole. It is through that determination and an undeterred tenacity that those persistent projects will inevitably emerge in their final result.

It may not be a walk in the woods nor the resonance of last night's dreams that inspire, but rather the immediacy of experienced life that makes it to the page itself. For a blank page resides as an insult to one's creative instinct, its unfulfilled lines mocking the writer, a psychological staredown taunting a call to action. It can be immediately resolved via the sensual stain of ink into page, creating footsteps of record and imagination preserved forever more, quickly attacking that contentious staredown.

In keeping, do not let the infinite distractions of life be an excuse not to live. Do not become a martyr laid to waste by the myriad beckonings of the trivial. For we are the authors of our stories, the grand architects of our lives, and must not fall sway to the mass hysterias of the collective that promote infinite entertainments, mindless distractions, and continuous follies.

So as we navigate the infinite labyrinth of possibilities in Milwaukee, in our art as well as in our lives, hard-won bravery and formed tactical sense should continually be wrought by consistent conscious effort. Fear of completion must be decimated by immediate action. Perfectionism is a false angel, an imposition mercilessly deposited into the depths of our unconscious to our ultimate detriment. We, if we are to succeed, must retaliate at all costs against those demons of deceit to regain our original ambitions and obliterate our received fears.

We must protect ourselves from the constant maelstrom of folly, to regulate the mind to create smooth thoroughfares of meaningful thought, to secure the borders of one's well-being against random conversations, distracting events, and abject foolishness, for our truest art, our greatest art, remains the design of our very own lives.

Even as you read this, the mystery of our existence continues to unravel into its unknown destiny, onto distant shores of the yet to be, that far-off horizon that will never actually be reached—because if dreams are to survive, they require the lure of the infinite. In Milwaukee those dreams persist . . .

You're Falling Down on the Job

MATT COOK

(*Originally published in* antinarrative journal.)

You're falling down on the job—
You fail to mention the trees laughing at you over by the water tower—
When everyone's depending on you,
To chronicle the trees laughing over by the water tower.

At issue is the window of time wherein pita bread maintains acceptable freshness.

The finger pointing and the finger painting
Have the potential to move beyond painting and pointing,
Into a transcendent place, where the dead are buried,
Across from the octopus car wash.

You bought salmon, asparagus, heavy whipping cream, the *New York Times*, red onions, Diet Pepsi,
And you watched the sunlight twinkle in a substandard puddle by the courthouse.

Right when you think there are no more distractions,
Along comes a distraction, and suddenly
You're muddling through muck that's actually worth muddling through muck for.

Chardi Kala: Reflections on Family, Terror, and Purpose after the Oak Creek Sikh Temple Shooting

PARDEEP KALEKA

I vividly remember the last time I saw my father alive. Before the spasm of violence in a place of worship, before the unthinkable lessons on pain, judgment, and humanity. The color of the memory of the last time I saw my father alive is amplified by the occasion being celebrated, my thirty-sixth birthday.

We gathered at my cousin Gary's place in Franklin, Wisconsin, for a family get-together and dinner. About fifty people showed up. Family is family and we make no discrepancy between brothers, sisters, cousins, the closeness of any relations. This way, we strive to embrace even strangers as family. We arrived to the party a bit late, but this was customary. In fact, we have a name for it: "Indian people time." Looking back, I guess we had a pretty valid excuse. My wife, Jaspreet, was about seven months pregnant, and our two little ones were simply not cooperating in terms of getting dressed up for this occasion.

Aside from all of this, we still arrived to the family function before my mother and father did. This was typical because my mother loved to get all dressed up for family get-togethers. My father, on the other hand, was never one to worry about his wardrobe. I assumed that he probably just arrived home from work and came over. Dad was a workaholic and this typically allowed time for only a short shower, grabbing a shirt from the top of the pile. The most attention was given toward tying his turban. It usually took him five minutes to take a shower and get dressed, but he used a meticulous ten minutes to tie his turban.

Once my wife and I arrived at my cousin's house, everyone reported to their predetermined posts. Our kids joined all of the other children, who were playing makeshift games already in progress. My wife, not one for gossip, joined in the gossip with the women, who were busy telling the latest about kids and family, with an occasional eye on the playing children. I reported to the men's den in Gary's basement. Every Punjabi house is purchased with these types of gatherings in mind. Where will the party be? Where will the children play without bothering the adults? Where will the women host? Most importantly, where will the men gather, and be out of earshot from their wives' probing curiosity?

I had been to Gary's place many times, so I knew that the guys would all gather in his finished basement. It is a very warm and inviting basement and as I walked down the stairs, I could already hear the conversation in progress between my uncles and cousins. I knew that they would be drinking and that they would probably have a huge plate of tandoori chicken. This is a type of chicken which is specially marinated, then cooked in a tandoori grill. The customary drink of choice with Punjabi men is whiskey and water, maybe a bit of ice, customarily called a "Punjabi Peg." A "peg" refers to the size of the drink, and Punjabi men who want to distinguish that this drink is unique only to us have lovingly coined this term to make it such. However, the only thing unique about this drink is that it has a larger alcohol content than your normal mixed drink. If a "normal peg" in India had 1/4 alcohol content, then a "Punjabi Peg" would have 1/2 alcohol content. It is safe to say that Punjabi men pride themselves in being able to have a few stiff ones. I have become very accustomed to this drink, so much so that I no longer suffer from hangovers when I drink it. In fact, I have never suffered from hangovers when I only drink this mixture. However, when I mix this with other drinks, then this calls for a tough night and an even tougher morning. Part of this is because whiskey has been the drink of choice for so many generations of Kaleka men. As far as I can remember, this was the drink that so many generations of us have indulged in. They were all very loyal men, so they did not stray from this preference. We are very loyal people, and it's no different with our drink. In a weird kind of way, you can say that this drink was in my heredity, in our heredity.

My uncles generally did the honor of pouring the drinks. It is their way of showing respect and love at the same time. As I accepted the honor of the first drink poured by my uncle, I raised a glass to toast the occasion of getting together, to "being healthy, wealthy, and wise." After my toast, no matter where they were in their drink, they said "cheers" and we all clinked our glasses together to signify the not-so-glorious meeting of the minds.

Everyone there was a small business owner, so during the discussion each person reflected on the aspects of his own business. Most of my family owned gas stations, liquor stores, convenience stores, and taxi cabs. Most of our conversations are centered around the fact that business is not as good as it should be, or not as good as in years past. I added little to the conversation because I was no longer focused in that line of business, though once in a while they turned to ask me about teaching inner city youth.

Eventually, my father made it downstairs. He was semi-dressed up, but his turban was in perfect shape. He had a way of tying his turban, which made him look much taller and more regal than others. Although he took a lot of pride in his ability to tie a turban, he made it seem like he did it effortlessly. It was like one of his favorite lines, "ko budhi gul ne hai," which translates to, "it's not a big deal." In fact, I don't remember him ever thinking or saying that anything was a big deal or that anything was impossible. Through the basement, he walked over and sat across from me, in between my uncles, in his own chair. He wished us all hello, which is done by closing our palms together, pointing our fingers to the sky, and saying "sat sri akal," which translates to "God is truth." We do this both when saying hello and when saying goodbye, so we might say this ten to twenty times per day.

My uncle poured dad a Punjabi Peg, while my father was telling him to take it easy on the whiskey. Dad had this semi-strict rule of only having one or two drinks with company. He didn't drink otherwise. My grandfather had this same rule. I had never seen my father drink outside of social occasions. However, my mother would tell me after Dad's death that he drank occasionally alone a few times to relieve stress. Other days during this week, I later learned, he had drank alone in the house. For Dad, the stress he faced was from religious politics. Dad had been President of the Sikh Temple of Wisconsin for fifteen years and many who were clamoring for increased power felt that it was his time to be relieved from this position. Many Sikh Temples around the world suffer from these type of politics and power plays.

Dad joined in our conversation about the struggles of businesses. His personal struggles with small business were a thing of the past. His relatable stories about business operation were from the eighties and nineties and everyone knew that. They knew that he was successful, and they understood that he was successful because he worked harder than anyone they had ever known. Further, he had worked harder than anyone I have ever heard of. But Dad never passed up the chance to offer sage advice, which generally made him the most talkative person at the party. I used to think that this was because he just enjoyed the sound of his own voice, but later I discovered he just had that much wisdom and love to share. He wanted to make sure that his community would thrive, which also explained why he served as the Temple President for so long. Dad typically started by talking about business, though he would steer the conversation to address bigger issues, like politics, family, and faith. He felt if we had a good foundation with these more critical issues, then the business, money, and economic side would all fall into place. As the conversations got "deeper," my voice got smaller. There were too many discussions being had that were lost in translation, and other topics where I felt out of step with the other men in the room.

I joined in the next round of drinks, as Dad slowly sipped his first one. Once my uncle poured me a third one, my father felt it was his duty to step in. He warned me about drinking and the discipline that is expected when participating in any vice. He didn't say this in a mean way, more as a matter of fact. We were all having a good time, and he didn't want to ruin it. I finished that drink, my last one for the evening.

By then dinner was ready and the entire family convened in the kitchen and living room. Everyone was abuzz, the men partly because they were buzzed, and the women because they got their gossip time in. I thanked my cousin's wife for hosting. Humbly, she stated, "it's no big deal." My wife and kids were all around, and everyone was either eating or getting ready to eat. The men would be the last to eat that night. I remember this meal being really, really good. After dinner, with kids antsy for my birthday cake, we quickly gathered around the table. Everyone joined in for a rendition of the happy birthday song. Wasn't I too old for this? Jai, my son who was four at the time, and Amaris, my six-year-old daughter, stood around me. They grinned from ear to ear as their father was serenaded by the whole family. I let them both blow out the candles. My father, the eldest and essentially the head of the family, cut the cake and went first in feeding me a slice. Ever the improviser, he cut cake with a knife, then used that same utensil to feed it to me, as if it was a fork. My mother joked to him, "You're going to cut our boy." I knew that I was not going to get cut. I also knew that that joke was her showing she cared.

The rest of the night was a bit of a blur. I think the liquor was catching up to me. I do remember my father giving his two grandbabies piggyback rides on the carpet in the living room. I remember a genuine glow of happiness from my pregnant wife.

These are the last living memories I have of my father. I am happy to say, during these last memories that he was truly "alive." Two days later, August 5 happened.

***

A beautiful sunny summer Sunday morning. The kids and I were sleeping in. Jaspreet woke up early and went into work to finish reports that were due on Monday. She was leaving for New York the next day. She went in early so that we could enjoy a family Sunday afternoon together; I had the same intention with a few errands to finish up by the afternoon. Eventually, both of our kids came into the room and asked the typical, "where is mom?" I explained to them that she had gone into work, but she shouldn't be long; I always said this to them, though today I truly meant it.

Amaris had a Punajbi class during Sunday school at the Gurdwara (Temple), where I was also going to drop off Jai to play with his cousins. There was always a built-in network of family at the Gurdwara, and I knew that all I had to do was get them both there so that family and fellow parishioners could watch them for me while I ran my errands. Many parents who had a few errands to run would use this same technique of "Sikh Sangat supervision." I brushed their teeth, washed them up, and got them dressed.

Amaris moved slowly, complaining about having to attend Sunday school. She couldn't find anything she liked to wear, she couldn't get her hair to look right, she had to get her socks to go on her feet the perfect way. The perfect way for her was with the crease of the sock going perfectly over her toes, as if she was modeling socks for a magazine shoot. I had to intervene at this point, because Jai was already dressed and ready to go. He, on the other hand, did not care how he looked. He didn't care about what he is wearing, wasn't concerned about his hair, and he didn't even care if he had socks on, let alone how perfect they looked. It took him five minutes from start to finish, while it took Amaris five minutes just for her socks to look proper. I have concluded that she is either a perfectionist or suffers from a mild case of OCD, probably both.

I knew that I needed to run these errands; however, I also wanted to pay my respects at the Gurdwara, which would require me to go inside for a while, do my greetings, and say a small prayer before I left. Gurdwara refers to the Sikhs' house of prayer, and the literal translation of the word "Guru" stands for teacher, and the word "Dwara" stands for door. The formal name of our Gurdwara was the Sikh Temple of Wisconsin. "Sikh" can be translated to "learner." Sikhism is a religion where teaching and learning, and learning and teaching are the basis for life. This being the case, until then I had personally never found this to be true of our Gurdwara. Obviously, I had learned to meditate and sit still for long periods of time, which maybe were valuable life skills. But I never really understood the true meaning of what was to be thought. This was partially my fault; I wasn't as fluent as I should be in the Punjabi language. This is why it was important for me to get Amaris to Sunday school. My hope was that she could develop that understanding and appreciation, as well as learn our native language, which had become not so native in my own urgency to assimilate to the American melting pot.

We left about quarter after 10:00 a.m. for her 11:00 a.m. class. This allowed me a comfortable period to get her situated and to do what I had to do in my obligatory prayer. Amaris was lollygagging and carrying on about the condition of her clothes, so we were still in a rush. A few minutes into our drive, we had to turn back around because she had forgotten a notebook for class. We were definitely running late, but once we were on our way in our second attempt to reach the Gurdwara, my mind was wandering to a basketball tournament the day before, to the tunes playing from my phone.

As we approached the roadway exit for the temple, police squad cars from different jurisdictions raced past our vehicle. I pulled to the shoulder, and thought they were driving dangerously. Back on the road, I saw they were driving the same direction as me, and then we came across other officers, rerouting traffic.

To one of the officers, I said, "Good Morning! Just wondering how I can get to the temple. The only way I know is through Howell Avenue?" The officer responded, "Sorry, we are not allowing anyone access to the temple right now. There has been a shooting and the scene is not secured yet." The officer said this with all of the clarity in the world. Still, I replied with, "What?" I didn't want to believe him. I wanted him to say something different. He didn't say anything different. He told me that "it just occurred ten minutes ago, and we need to stay clear of the intersection." I thought about Amaris taking so long getting ready, forgetting her notebook. What would we have walked into if we had showed up on time?

And what about everyone who was there? I knew Mom was at the temple because she always got there early to help prepare food for the day. Dad was there early to help a new immigrant family raise desperately needed money to get on their feet. The officer listened as I explained that my family was inside that temple. He had concerns of his own, he said—securing the scene of a mass shooting. My heart was inside the temple and my children were still in the back seat of the car. I kept the car parked at that intersection and minutes later I began to receive phone calls. One call after another. Family and friends telling me that there had been a shooting at the Gurdwara, asking me where my parents were or if I had talked with them. One call would end, another one would come through. Then, a call from my father's phone. But on the other line was the head priest. He didn't speak any English, though I understood his Punjabi. My father had been shot, he said. It was serious and he needed help right away.

Next, my wife called and said that my mother was trying to get a hold of me. Mom was hiding in a closet inside the kitchen of the temple. With all of the other calls to me, my mother had been getting a busy signal. And in the midst of all of this commotion, I realized that my kids were sitting in the back seat of the car, listening to all of this on the Bluetooth speaker. Jai, visibly angry, said to me, "Dad, I will get the bad guys." Amaris was crying. I took the speaker off and comforted my kids. Extended family and other members from the temple began to arrive at the same intersection. They asked me questions; I handed over Amaris and Jai and said that I'd be back.

I had to do something . . . but what? So I went over to my cousin, who had just arrived. The two of us made our way past the sight of police and conjured a plan to go through the woods and fields in the back of Howell Avenue all the way to the temple. This path would take forever, so we turned back to the officers to ask if they could help us reach the temple. "I will arrest you if you go near the scene." Couldn't this officer tell that this was not a damn scene to us? I thought back to my past career of policing and wondered if I was that insensitive. But this was our heart being attacked.

More of our family, including my wife, gathered in a tavern parking lot as close as we could get to the temple at the time. I told them what I knew, they briefed us on what they were aware of. Calls from inside the temple kept coming in. On the other line, my mother whispered, "I'm okay, but we are all inside the pantry in the kitchen. Please tell them to help us." I asked if she knew anything about Dad. She said she didn't because when they heard the gunshots, they all ran into the pantry. Why would someone do this, and what could I do? Dear God, I'm desperate! I saw my brother fall to his knees and begin to pray. Media focused their cameras on us at a time when we were at our most vulnerable. How had our life become their entertainment? People were talking to me, but their words didn't make any sense. This whole thing didn't make any sense.

As the kids got picked up, we were still trying to keep contact with my mom, who continued to whisper that she and all of the ladies in the closet were fine, but she was also asking if we had spoken to Dad. I felt like she knew something terrible had happened to him. Sometimes, lovers can truly feel each other's pain. My wife kept calm, one of her unique abilities, as she repeatedly called Dad's phone, reaching the head priest each time. When we asked him to put our father on the phone, he told us that he couldn't. I feared the worst. I contacted an old partner on the Milwaukee Police force to see if he could help us get any closer to the scene. He said he was aware of what was taking place. He shared the site of the Command Post (CP) and had me describe the layout of the building and what I had heard about the situation inside. I give him my mother's phone number, reluctantly, as I didn't know if she was in a safe place to talk.

The CP was in the parking lot across the street. Squad cars and paramedics lined the inside of the law enforcement barricades. Now the sight was joined by many media outlets, local, national, international. The Salvation Army and American Red Cross had arrived. Our community was on the outside looking in to the crime scene. People were lined up for blocks. There were a mixture of emotions: confusion, anger, sadness, fear. This was the most ominous sight I have ever seen.

Through old police contacts, I finagled my way into the scene parking lot across the street from the temple. Officers told me that there were members of the Gurdwara who were inside while the shooting was taking place and that they had been escorted into a nearby bowling alley. I made my way inside the bowling alley to hopefully find my parents. Inside, my mother was crying hysterically on the floor. I picked her up, and told her that she was fine, that she was safe. Once I finally got her to calm down, her attention went to my father. She asked me if I had heard from him. Obviously I had not, I had only spoken to the priest, on my Dad's phone. I told her this, and as soon as I did, we were ushered into a conference area where the authorities were conducting interviews. They needed interpreters to conduct many of the interviews so I volunteered. More information was coming out now: that the shooter was white, an avowed "white supremacist." Most people in our community didn't know what a white supremacist was or anything about their ideological beliefs.

Once the interview with Mom was done, I also relieved myself of my duty to translate. My urgency was to find out what happened to Dad. Eventually, I found the head priest standing against a wall. In Punjabi, he said, "Your dad was shot. I picked up the phone and was calling you because I don't know how to speak English." I asked him if he saw Dad alive or was he dead, in which time he said again, "He was shot, and I heard him praying and calling out for help." He told me that he himself was hiding in the bathroom when dad was shot, and that he stayed in the bathroom because he was scared. He handed Dad's cell phone to me. I wanted so badly for this phone to be my father instead. It is amazing how much some of our possessions can represent us.

In the group of people comforting each other, including my mother, was one of the women who was shot at by the gunmen. She had narrowly escaped into the pantry with my mother. I knew their son, who was an FBI agent; we grew up together, partied together, had followed similar career paths. Our families were close though we had drifted apart. The husband of the woman who was shot at was a powerful temple trustee, a key player in the establishment of the Gurdwara in Oak Creek. Amid the conversation, he said that my dad had been transported to the hospital. Must be good news, I thought, because he'd be getting medical attention.

By now, more and more family had made their way into the basement. My wife, aunties, and uncles were all here comforting us. Even my old partner from the police force was there. We began contacting every hospital in the area, enlisting our family full of doctors, to locate Dad. No luck. Someone said he might have gone to the hospital and been released. I said: "I know Dad, and if he went to the hospital and was released, he would have come back to the Gurdwara." I know how much Dad loved his community, and if he could, he wouldn't be anywhere else but with his community.

I decided that I needed to talk to someone else who might know more about the situation and, possibly, my dad. Rumors circulated in the basement that one of the families there had seen a loved one murdered inside the temple. I approached this family. They all had the look of loss and were not talking at all. I mustered up the courage to introduce myself and began a conversation by asking if they were okay, if they needed anything. They all gave me an obligatory, "We are fine," in Punjabi. A little girl in the family made eye contact with me as if she had something she wanted to tell me. Her mother gave me permission to talk with the little girl alone. I began with some simple dialogue. The little girl told me her name and that they had come from India about a month before the shooting. She told me that her father was now dead. I ask her how she knew. She told me that she, her brother, and mom had seen him dead with their own eyes. Her father was a priest that was sponsored by my dad. He had been in the United States for some time, maybe ten years. He must have finally gotten his clearance to bring his family to the States.

The girl told me exactly what she had seen. She and her brother were in the storage room next to the temple kitchen, watching an Indian police drama on TV, a show called *C.I.D.* At about 10:30 a.m., they heard gunshots, but the sounds were faint so they thought it must be part of the television show. Next, her father knocked on the door, handed her the keys for the basement and insisted that they immediately go downstairs and find safety. From the sound of her father's voice, something serious was going on.

She, her brother, and mother ran downstairs with another ten or so people while they heard the gunshots taking place upstairs. Kids and grown-ups were panicked and crying. After about a half-hour, she decided with her mom, her brother, and another woman to go upstairs and check on their father. Just inside the main hall, they saw a woman lying in a pool of blood. They turned around and saw the head priest, the same man who had been answering my dad's phone, who told them that their father was in the far bedroom with two other people. To get to that bedroom, they walked past another body of an elderly man who was not breathing and lying in a pool of blood. A little farther, the girl said she saw her father also lying in a pool of blood, unresponsive. He was missing an eye and we would later discover that he was shot point blank in the head by the shooter. Her mother was hysterical and begged for her husband to wake up. The girl touched her father's injured eye; she got his blood on her finger, which frightened her.

She saw one other body lying on the ground and then the head priest told them to "find somewhere to hide and stay there." Her entire family went into a bathroom, with the body of her dad and the other man just outside of their locked door. Inside the bathroom, they heard another voice. It was my father's voice, and he was praying, repeating the word "waheguru." Waheguru is a Sikh word for "God," "Supreme Being." She told me that she heard his voice for about ten minutes and then it stopped.

After about an hour, the police knocked on the door and ordered them out of the bathroom with their hands in the air. When she came out, she said my father's body wasn't there. The police led them all outside, put them into cars, and transported them across the street to the bowling alley.

She apologized for not having more information. I was sorry for what her innocent mind had to endure. I thought to myself that when a daughter calls out to her father because she is scared, a father should always be able to comfort her. Obviously, now, her father could not.

Back in the bowling alley, my mother was screaming to find her husband. There was too much confusion, too many conflicting stories. I had lost hope in our law enforcement by then. It was hard to know who to trust. It felt as if we were not really the priority. I wondered if this would have been different if the parishioners were white churchgoers instead of immigrant Sikhs. I wondered if the response would have been different if the shooter was a brown man instead of a white man. I still wonder this today.

Meanwhile, my brother, Amardeep, relayed information to us from the media. Amardeep was doing his best considering the circumstances, and I knew he would put on a brave face for the world despite our pain. By now, reports were being released that there had been seven fatalities, one being the shooter, identified as a white supremacist who was shot and killed by a police officer on the scene. Lieutenant Brian Murphy, the responding officer, had been shot numerous times and escorted to the hospital. The Oak Creek Police Chief labeled the attack domestic terrorism.

By evening, much of the crowd had dispersed, and I decided that I needed fresh air. It was near dusk outside as I walked to the edge of the barrier to look at the Gurdwara. I saw my father's pick-up truck. Amardeep walked up next to me. He looked tired. We didn't say anything to each other, as we had been in constant communication all day. I was proud of him, as he stood in front of the glaring eyes of the world and demonstrated courage, and "chardi kala," which in our culture means "relentless optimism, even in the face of tragedy." After about twenty minutes, we broke our silence.

He said to me, "Are you thinking what I'm thinking?"

I replied, "Yes, Dad is no longer with us."

I wanted more than anything to have been able to comfort my dad. I thought about all of the good times we shared. I recalled the bad ones, too. It's amazing how much your mind can process in a short amount of mindful time. I wanted to go back in time, and listen more to what he said, and I wished that I wouldn't have been so argumentative. Amardeep reflected, too, and neither one of us talked, as we lived out our dwindling hopes.

Later, the two of us were summoned to the office inside of the bowling alley. When I was policing, I had to make these types of notifications and now I sat on the receiving end of what seemed like inevitable bad news.

My ears rang and I was extremely angry. Plainly, the police officer told me that Dad was one of the victims of the shooting. Everything after that was a blur. I looked at the officer as if I could jump into his body and make it explode from the inside out. All of my frustrations with today glared at him. I didn't see the humanity in this police officer and it was taking all of me not to strike out. I sat there and listened, teeth clenched, hands sweating, heart racing. I forgot Amardeep was next to me. What took so long . . . how long did Dad suffer before actually passing . . . could anyone have been saved . . . could it have been handled differently . . . why did I get into that last fight with Dad? We walked out, Amardeep was crying, I was pissed. I told him that I would meet him at home, I didn't want anyone to drive with me. I wanted to be alone. I got to my car and I thought, they are all cowards. The shooter's a coward for attacking the most devout and faithful at their house of sanctuary. Law enforcement personnel were cowards for keeping us in the dark and not having the courage to notify my mother. Now that was left up to me when I got home. Society itself was a bunch of cowards for their complacency.

I screamed in the loneliness of my car all of the way home. This was the only way I mustered up the courage to tell Mom. When I arrived home, I was tired from screaming. I saw my family all gathered outside, as if they were scared to go into the house. They were all waiting on me. How would I do this, how would I tell her? The door opened and as I walked in, my mom looked at me. I couldn't say anything, I couldn't get a word out. Lord. Mom stared at me and fell to the floor sobbing. Amardeep and I ran over to her and held her. I felt others holding us as we all cried on the floor.

That would not be the last day I cried and that would not be the last day that others have held me. My tears and feelings come on spontaneously. Sometimes I'm in a car, sometimes at events. There is no rhyme or reason to nostalgia.

Since the shooting, our community has attempted to return to normalcy, whatever that is. Most of the families have gone back to the temple but there are always challenges in reclaiming sanctuary.

I am personally driven by this challenge of fostering healing and sanctuary, whether it is inside our place of worship or within our communities. The past six years sometimes seem to have gone by so fast and yet at other times have felt so slow. During this process—and it is indeed a process—I have learned that my best medicine is honesty. I could not run from my wounds, I could not escape them, I could not avoid nor dilute them. I had to and still have to face these wounds. For these wounds have purpose. I was told a long time ago that "time heals all." This is not exactly true. What is true is that time, consciousness, forgiveness, and purpose can help heal. My children are healthy, they live with the understanding that their grandfather was a martyr for a far bigger cause then himself. They work hard to pave their own legacy and appreciate the responsibility they each have to this country.

We should not be so judgmental of the journey each one takes, but instead honor the pain of that journey. There is a legacy in this honor, and it is in this legacy that we will all create a world that promises to be better than the one we inherited.

Alchemy

JUDE GENEREAUX

Alchemy: a mingling; the medieval chemical science, object of which was to transmute base metals into gold, to discover the universal cure for disease and means of indefinitely prolonging life.

A frosty New Year's morning
from a corner window, our favorite room
we watch the Calatrava salute
a new morning sun.

Sea smoke rolls off Lake Michigan,
the famous blue flame flags our cold walk
to the Plaza for coffee & eggs & early chatter.
Streets lined with brownstone mansions,
gothic churches, and cafes steeped
in the scent of the old country.
We wander through bookstores
the riverfront; the Oriental at two o'clock.

City lights dot & glitter the night sky as our
cab delivers us to the warmth of golden lobbies
beckoning "come inside";
Pfister's piano man teases longing and
memory from ivory & shadow
the tower turns, blue jazz on top.

We begin again
open as Calatrava's wings.

STATE OF
THE ARTS

Milwaukee Breakwater Lighthouse by Luke Chappelle

Mixed Feelings at City Hall by Luke Chappelle

Milorganite by Luke Chappelle

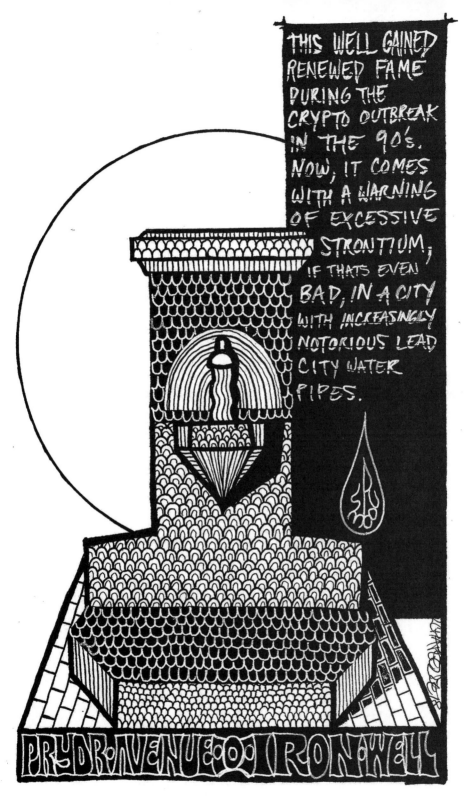

THIS WELL GAINED RENEWED FAME DURING THE CRYPTO OUTBREAK IN THE 90's. NOW, IT COMES WITH A WARNING OF EXCESSIVE STRONTIUM, IF THATS EVEN BAD, IN A CITY WITH INCREASINGLY NOTORIOUS LEAD CITY WATER PIPES.

PRYOR·AVENUE·o·IRON·WELL

Pryor Avenue Iron Well by Luke Chappelle

168

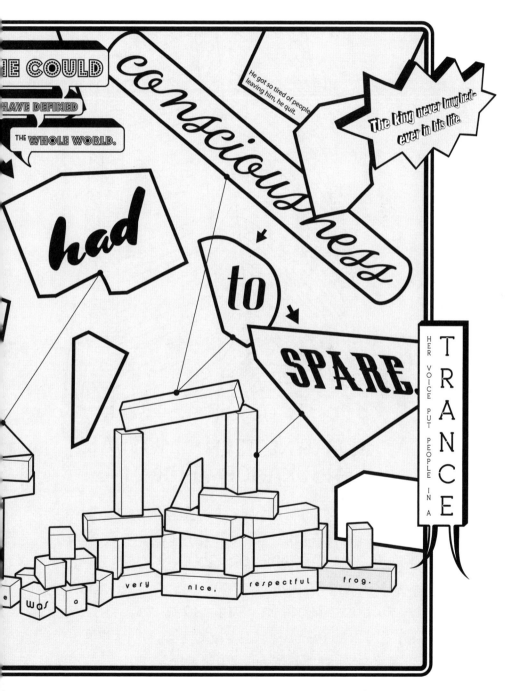

Sherman Park by Reginald Baylor

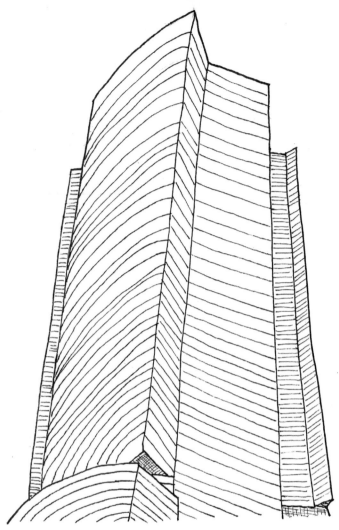

NORTHWESTERN MUTUAL INSURANCE BUILDING

A GLASS DOWNTOWN SKYSCRAPER IN A CITY DEVOID OF NEW, TALL BUILDINGS FOR A DECADE OR SO. NOW THE SECOND-TALLEST IN THE CITY, WHICH WOULD MAKE IT THE 32ND-TALLEST BUILDING IN CHICAGO. (BUT LET'S NOT GET INTO CHICAGO.)

Northwestern Mutual HQ by Dug Belan

THE FORTRESS

A BOOT-AND-TANNERY TURNED WEIRDO ARTIST LOFTS TAKES ITS NEXT TURN AS A TRENDY APARTMENT-AND-OFFICE DEVELOPMENT.

The Fortress by Dug Belan

THE DORMANT, LOOMING "OLD MAIN" SOLDIER'S HOME
WILL GET CITY AND DEVELOPER AID TO
HOPEFULLY HOUSE HOMELESS VETERANS.

Soldier's Home by Dug Belan

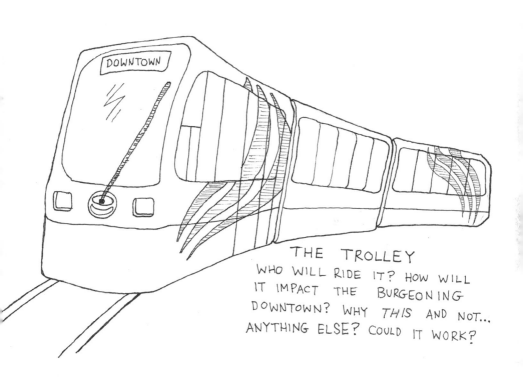

THE TROLLEY
WHO WILL RIDE IT? HOW WILL
IT IMPACT THE BURGEONING
DOWNTOWN? WHY *THIS* AND NOT...
ANYTHING ELSE? COULD IT WORK?

The Street Car by Dug Belan

OUT THERE

Living Like Kings

CATHERINE LANSER

I am sure if you cut into me you would find pink flaky flesh that could easily be lifted away with a salad fork. I read that 90 percent of the protein in the brown bears of Alaska was once salmon. I would estimate my percentage of Lake Michigan salmon to be nearly as high.

Unlike the salmon swimming there, I am a native of Lake Michigan. I was born on its shores in Port Washington, Wisconsin, when there was an endless supply of salmon just within reach. Day after day my six brothers, like fisherman on the Sea of Galilee, backed our avocado-green Crestliner into the lake, catching enough fish to feed a village, but bringing them home for my family of nine children and two parents.

Rows and rows of the salmon's pink flesh, chopped harshly into chunks, stood ready in Mason jars on our root cellar shelf. It was eaten both hot and cold in a loop of recipes. Other times the jars were popped open and the salmon was eaten just like that. My brother Rick recalls throwing jars into the boat to eat while they fished. On top of the water he scooped hunks of salmon flesh from the jar with his hands while his line waited beneath to lure more into the boat.

We ate it formed into hot loaves covered with a gelatinous gravy of peas or molded into patties served on hamburger buns. When we were celebrating birthdays, Christmases, or graduations, it was smoked whole and split open so we could tear it right off the bone to eat on soda crackers. When we were feeling more continental, we ate it pureed together with cream cheese and a mysterious substance called Liquid Smoke on fancier store-brand Ritz crackers.

I never fished for it myself, but if you asked me, I would have guessed that all you needed to do was dip your hand in the water to pull out another salmon. My brothers would come home and hold their catch up by the mouths for admiration and to be rewarded with, "That's a nice looking Chinook," or, "How big is that coho?"

I stood next to them in the driveway as my mom snapped their pictures. My four- or five-year-old body was used for scale to show that the fish was nearly my size. On our busy street, which ran between the high, middle, and elementary schools, someone always drove by and honked their horn and nodded in approval.

At the time I didn't know that coho and Chinook were different types of salmon, or that salmon wasn't native to the Great Lakes. Later I would find out that it had been introduced, beginning in the late 1960s, before I was born. The fish were stocked to create sport fishing on the Great Lakes, save the nearly extinct trout and waning whitefish population, and to hunt the abhorrent alewife, a fish that isn't as fun as its name would imply. To me it sounded like the kind of spouse a man who likes to drink beer could take with him to the tavern. Instead of goodtime girls, these turned out to be rather stinky fish that washed up on the slim beaches of our town in great number to rot in the sun.

Over the years the salmon prospered, assisted along by the Department of Natural Resources (DNR) personnel who collected the eggs and ensured that they matured at fish hatcheries before returning them to the lakes. As the population grew, so did fishing for sport and my town's harbor, from a simple boat launch into a full-scale marina that would eventually house graceful sailboats, luxury yachts big enough to fit kitchens and sleeping areas, and charter boats to take those who could pay the price to look for Chinook, the king of the salmon.

Though our plentiful natural resource had begun to transform our town into a cute little fishing village "just twenty minutes north of Milwaukee," we were slow to notice it. The lake was inaccessible for the most part, except by boat. The marina and its piers were closed off to those who didn't own the large boats parked there. A path past the wastewater treatment plant led to the only beach where you might swim if the water wasn't so icy and inhospitable. The rest of the shoreline had been eroded by the force of the lake's water, current, and winds, leaving a jagged and steep cliff that was nice for houses to perch above, but not for people to access the water below.

My family gave up stockpiling salmon a long time ago, but it still comes up in conversation. A few years back my brother served smoked fish at his own daughter's graduation. I scraped some flesh from the bones and placed it on a cracker before popping it in my mouth and savoring the smoky, salty taste.

"This is good smoked salmon," I said.

He shook his head, "It's smoked trout."

"Maybe that's why it's so good," another brother said. We all laughed.

I had barely eaten salmon since the last jar was opened in my mom's kitchen. I avoided it on menus when dining out and never cooked it at home, remembering it as something watery and greyish-pink from my past. Today, discussions revolve around days gone by, or chatting about its health benefits with any number of tablemates who tout its high Omega-3 content as they order it from the menu. It seems now you can fill a whole conversation discussing the many facets of its health benefits. When I tell friends how plentiful salmon was in my childhood, they tell me how lucky I was. I put my hand out flat and flap it up and down, "Maybe, maybe not."

These days when I exit the highway and drive into Port Washington, the lake looks much different to me. As I turn the corner toward downtown, it spreads out before me on the horizon forever. Now instead of taking the shortcut, I drive the long way, down the main drag. When I look toward downtown, at the corner of Franklin Street and Grand Avenue, where Port Washington's two main streets meet, the skyline has changed, too.

For most of my life, a large decapitated metal giraffe stood on a peninsula reaching out into the lake. Beneath it, an 18,000-ton black mountain of coal was deposited monthly for seventy-two years. But now the power plant, though still puffing smoke into the air, no longer runs on that fossil fuel. It was converted to natural gas in 2005. The gigantic headless coal bridge was dismantled almost a decade later and replaced with a park and a bird sanctuary. Now, I can get closer to the water than ever before. Walking out on this expanse of land, I can't imagine a more inappropriate spot to store the poisonous chemical.

Coal releases sulfur dioxide into the air as well as nitrogen oxides. The first causes respiratory illness, the second causes acid rain and ground-level ozone. After I left home and talked about my childhood, I would ask others if they remembered the "ozone warnings" as I did, when we were told to stay inside because of high ozone content in the air. My lungs would ache when I rode my bike or played in the park behind our house, having ignored the warnings.

When coal is burned, the mercury which naturally occurs inside it is sent into the air and eventually ends up in our bodies of water. Once there, microorganisms change mercury into methylmercury which eventually ends up in the fish. Methylmercury levels grow up the food chain to larger fish that live longer lives. Babies born to pregnant women who eat fish exposed to methylmercury are at greater risk of cerebral palsy, mental retardation, low birth weight, and early sensorimotor dysfunction. It was just one of the pollutants that caused Illinois, Indiana, Wisconsin, and

Michigan, to issue a warning against eating more than one serving of fish caught in the Great Lakes by 1985.

Still, the growth continued with salmon fishing in the Great Lakes, to my own community, and others just like it along the shores. By 2009, coastal communities along Lake Michigan's shoreline earned $32 million from salmon fishing. This was despite the 1980s collapse of salmon fishing in Lake Michigan due to a bacterial kidney disease that killed off most of the fish and that caused anglers to start fishing in Lake Huron. Now the salmon population there has dwindled because of a reduction in the alewife population. Alewives died off because invasive species like zebra and quagga mussels had cleared the lake of plankton, the alewives' food source. As a result, local tourist communities found themselves in the red.

As these communities faltered, the focus on fishing shifted back to Lake Michigan. But in recent years, a decrease in alewife population has led to less food for salmon and dwindling populations for fishermen in Lake Michigan. The DNR stocks less salmon as the salmon now can reproduce on their own. Some say the alewife population has been controlled and that the day of the salmon may be done as trout populations have grown.

Smith Brothers Fish Shanty is no longer at the corner, where Port Washington's two main streets meet. The two-story restaurant was once nearly as big as a city block. The building was capped with a neon sign of a larger-than-life man carrying his catch home. He was dressed in a yellow rain slicker and sou'wester hat and was smoking a pipe. The fish draped over his shoulder was as large as his body and stretched all the way to his feet as he leaned into the wind and the letters of the sign. Outside murals showed similar men standing at the helm of a ship battling great waves. Inside, patrons used to order fish and cocktails in nautical-themed dining rooms that were decked out with life preservers and stuffed fish, nets hanging from the ceiling, and anchor lines tied around pillars.

It was the center of tourism for the city, but like the headless giraffe of the power plant, it too is gone. For a long time even after it closed, the neon sign stood tall, a reminder of the way things had been. But once when I returned home, the sign was gone, sold to a fishmonger in the public market in downtown Milwaukee, a new kind of tourist attraction, focused on healthful, artisanal food. I visited the market once and didn't even recognize the man in his new home.

Looking up Franklin Street, there are an attractive array of historical buildings that still bring people to town for a visit. I hadn't really thought much of them until I learned they were significant on a show highlighting tourism in my town. The bay window and turret of one building rounded out over one street corner, into the cornice near the sky on the next, and the curtain fluttering behind the arched window blended into the one after that. Rising above them is the city's most famous man-made attraction, St. Mary's Church, an 1850s Gothic-revival-style building towering atop a hill overlooking downtown. Because of the angle, it seems to stand in the middle of the road. Looking up at it, I can almost see what the tourist ads say about my town. Creamy brick and limestone merge with the sound of seagulls into a mosaic that transports me to a seaside town in the Northeast, one on the coast of the Atlantic, not a Great Lake.

But the memory of the headless giraffe lives on. When the salmon are no more, they will remain inside me, too.

Exchange Students: Rufus King and Kaukauna High Schoolers Present a Play

JOANNE WILLIAMS

In the spring of 2016, I found one of the only copies of my high school newspaper that I had saved. The story on the front page was from 1966. It was the story of an exchange of black and white high school students in Wisconsin.

In all my years of journalism, I have never felt as passionate about a story as I do about this one. Seeing the success of the exchange in 1966, I felt, could open people's eyes to new ways of relating to each other today. This exchange first happened in 1966 . . . right in the middle of the civil rights movement . . . fifty-plus years ago.

The schools were Rufus King High School in Milwaukee and Kaukauna High School up in the Fox River Valley. As part of the exchange, the students lived in each other's homes, went to each other's high school, and performed the groundbreaking play, *In White America*, in both schools.

This was the first time some of the Kaukauna students had ever seen black people in person. The first time the Milwaukee students, both black and white, had ever lived in a small, all-white town in central Wisconsin, nearly two hours from their homes and seemingly a world away.

As we experience confusing and depressing racial issues now, the story of a successful exchange between black and white high school students during the civil rights era needs to be brought to light. That is part of the reason I have started a documentary project into the collaboration and connections between these two schools . . . spotlighted by Kaukauna's invitation to the 2016 cast from Rufus King to show that community the play that started the exchange, fifty years earlier.

There were no auditions or competition between students in 1966 to participate in the exchange. The teachers, social studies teacher Thomas Schaffer at Kaukauna and English teacher Ruth Thomas, chose the students they thought would be able to handle the cultural exploration. They knew this would be much more than an educational exchange. The students in the sixties knew it, too.

Joe McCarty, a white student from Kaukauna, said, ". . . this exchange program proved to be the greatest thing of my high school years . . . being in this it really kind of tore away the bubble I was in as far as coming from a small town, Kaukauna . . . then moving into the inner-city . . ."

Allen Kemp, a black student from Rufus King, said, ". . . My homeroom teacher was a lady by the name of Ruth Thomas . . . here was a lady that was well ahead of her time. She was taking these little-bitty black kids at Rufus King High School and making them do things. They just didn't sit around . . ."

Since I began research in 2016, people have come forward with memories from fifty-plus years ago, and shared new opinions about racial understanding. As it turns out, I was part of the performances since I sang in the chorus. My family also hosted the students at a party in my basement. I discovered that memory when I came across some old black and white Polaroid pictures taken in our rec room in 1966. Through those audiences, we have seen how it related to people in Kaukauna today, and the story keeps expanding.

Every City with a Side

FREESIA MCKEE

Would you be happier paying $1,000 a month for a closet apartment and eating dried beans in a stranger's city? These are the questions I'm asking these days. Why are all these graphic designers moving to Thirty-fifth Street, Thirty-second Street, and Thirtieth Street in my city? The last bartender I met said my neighborhood of origin is a bad one. He said this two blocks from the apartment I live in now, which is good? Last year, a musician asked if I grew up in the ghetto or the good part. I said neither. What should I have said? How do you explain when all you've wanted to do is leave this city? How do you also stay proud?

This month, all the snow has melted and you can see a winter's worth of plastic bags caught in the bushes along the freeway, blowing like the flags of the houses that were demolished for it to be built there.

A long time ago, I met a student from New York City who seemed older than the rest of us. Our conversation ended when he said I would never "make it" in New York. I hadn't even said I wanted to try. It was puzzling because we were sixteen. Did he think he had "made it" by being born somewhere special?

I felt satisfied in my jealousy and its opposite when I found a poet who I realized wouldn't be able to "make it" in Milwaukee. We wouldn't be able to stroke his ego with local competition. We are just not that important. We are neighborhoods described in different ways. We ask too many questions at the Q and A. We are dirty snow, a tough crowd. It's just like anyplace else.

More in Store

MAA VUE

Growing up in Wisconsin, I have always heard my Hmong peers speak about the active community in Milwaukee. Like how they always have the bigger parties, a larger Hmong population, and that they just overall . . . had more in store.

I never got to experience any of it until I became a singer and songwriter in 2013. Wausau, where I live and work, is smack-dab in the middle of the state and about three hours from Milwaukee. The more music I made, I'd start to get bookings at small private parties, like weddings and family celebrations in Milwaukee. Other times, I would pass through on my way to the airport and then see the vast, big city from up in the sky.

It wasn't until 2016 that I got to take part in the Milwaukee community as the main headliner at the biggest annual Hmong New Year's celebration event in Wisconsin. Hmong New Year festivals in the United States are held between October and the end of December. Traditionally, the festivals celebrate the end of harvest and welcome the new year. Some of the things you'll experience at Hmong New Year festivals: you can smell that freshly steamed rice in the air along with scents like BBQ meats and spicy papaya salads being made; people bustling through shops, displaying the latest ethnic Hmong art, clothing, music, and movies; bright and festive colors, especially during singing and dance competitions and pageants.

The Milwaukee Hmong New Year festival was held in a huge warehouse-like square building that has a dividing wall down the middle to keep vendors on one side and the main stage on the other. This made it easy for attendees to maneuver, picking and choosing which side of fun they'd like to be on. Until my concert, I'd only seen online videos and photos that captured the night concert. And though it was jam-packed with attendees in prior years, I couldn't assume that it would be the same for me. So you can guess how nervous and anxious I was about people showing up for my night concert.

When I entered the building for my performance, I remember just keeping my head down to prevent me from being seen by the audience as security led me backstage. The stage crew and event coordinators were very accommodating and made sure my safety was intact. As I settled backstage,

I was running transition notes between songs in my head while my hands shook nervously.

As it was still early in the night, 7:00 p.m. to be exact, I peeked out from the back to get a glimpse of the audience and their atmosphere. I only saw a handful of people line-dancing in front of the stage to the music from the opening band. A huge spotlight blinded the view further past the front stage, so I assumed there were not enough people in attendance yet.

An hour later, a coordinator for the show told me that the audience was growing anxious and wanted to know when I would be performing. There wasn't a set schedule since there were only two openers and myself for the night. Knowing what I saw in attendance, I decided to wait it out for another hour.

Finally, the emcee announced my name on stage. The audience didn't make much noise, as I'm sure they couldn't hear clearly due to the bad reverb from the sound system in the warehouse. Once my music started playing and I made my way to the front stage in my hooded cape wardrobe, the screams and audience bustling became so loud that I almost lost my balance.

And that's when I felt it. The large abundance of adrenaline that raced through my body gave me the courage to look out into the audience after removing my hood. And my gosh, standing on the elevated stage, I was blown away by the hundreds of people in attendance that were backed all the way up to the dividing wall. It felt incredible. Even though I was performing in a divided square building, the crowd looked like it stretched for miles. I could see their awe-filled expressions and their eyes light up because they hadn't seen my kind of performance (wearing a cape, lol). They all rushed toward the stage like a Black Friday sale was about to happen. They were people wanting and looking to have a great time. That was the best part about performing for this audience. Their cheers, chants, and participation in singing along with me made it such a fun time. With this incredible welcome and support from the audience, it made the rest of the night easy breezy, and I couldn't help but feel like Milwaukee had become a new home for me.

As my performance came to an end, there was the last line in the last song that I changed and sang in the following way: "if only our love can be rewritten, have it begin . . . when we were in Milwaukee."

I felt like this last touch-up in the song wrapped up the overall vibe and time that the audience and I had felt during our short time together. I won't ever forget this experience in Milwaukee.

A Stand-Up Walks into a Bar

SAMMY ARECHAR

I take a lot of pride in being born and raised here, but every time someone asks me to recommend things to do when they visit, I sound very uncultured.

All I ever recommend are dive bars and the Quizno's in the airport. People want to know about the museums, the historical buildings, and what makes Milwaukee unique. When they hear me talk about what bars have free popcorn and which restaurants sell Tums, they look at me like a furniture store commercial: 0% interest.

However, after much thought, drinking is what makes Milwaukee so great. It's a big part of our culture and with all of the breweries and distilleries in the city alone, it is very much a huge part of our local economy. Also, I've noticed that everyone else kinda recommends drinking-related activities as well so I don't feel so bad about not sounding sophisticated by recommending any of our great bird sanctuaries or spaghetti luncheons.

One thing I really like about Milwaukee that doesn't get mentioned very often is how we have unique names for everyday things: ATMs are "Tyme Machines," water fountains are called "bubblers," and we call Michael Jackson the King of Soda. This is the only saving grace I have when I sing Milwaukee's praises to people looking to visit our city. Please feel free to use it when you want to end your list of recommendations; it would at least guarantee a lukewarm nod of the head.

I want to thank you for reading my installment in this book. I am very grateful to have been asked to write something about my hometown. I also want to apologize to the editor for me taking over a month to submit this. (My lack of recommendations and the fear of judgment from it was what took so long.)

Everything Bruce Lee at Seven Mile Fair in Orange

ROBERT EARL THOMAS

the night was . . . humid

Bruce Lee hadn't been dead eight years

at three years old i got my first dog at Seven Mile Fair

he was set in the middle of a spare tire in the gravel
for sale

he peed in the backseat on the way home
we named him Omashkooz
Ojibwe for elk hound
years later he was run over by a car
full circle.

prepped
the orange night, having broke
we'd station wagon from Thirty-seventh and Vliet
all the way to Seven Mile Fair on the outskirts of town
Five in the morning
when we got there dad would buy me styrofoam cup orange juice
and chocolate glazed donut
very eating sleepy this is early
weekend after weekend dark orange sky very cold
my first international experience of sorts

dad and grampa were weekend vendors
sitting on the bumper of the clay colored station wagon
all day drinking Billy beer
selling wrenches, gears, nuts, bolts, overalls, work shirts,
Nat King Cole and bing crosby 45's,
huge cheap wooden radios, brasso, all things oily;

to talk about the war.
haggling grampa said, "jew 'em down!"
the nearby men loved it and laughed.

the tops of my toes were scuffed and undone
bleeding always it seemed
dust from the parking lot an active coagulant thereon
kung fu theatre come alive in a flash
karate shoes all day, everyday

Bruce Lee
Bruce Lee on everything at the fair, throughout Milwaukee, really
Bob's Big Boy, Woolworths, Gift Land, EVERYWHERE
i'm saying Bruce Lee was everywhere in 1981.
Bruce Lee pocket calendars, posters, vanity mirrors, commemorative plates,
sunglasses,
knock offs, knock it offs

anyway, walked off and got me some nunchucks
mom said no, made me take 'em back,
but i had it in mind i was gonna be ching chong chang
a ninja star throwing
individually wrapped slice of American cheese eating
little fat ass, pepsi drinking super hero so and so.
alas, didn't happen.

ching chong chang another day, perhaps.
ching chong chang didn't even really exist
he was a construct of the automobile industry

sitting in the dirt underneath gramps's folding table
cousin and i unfold a language
punctuating gibberish jokes with laughs
my wonderheart constructing
before the Asian lady few times
at figh dolla figh dolla
sound good? you want it or not?

parrots, chickens, puppies,
carne asada, necklaces, speakers,
solvents, tires, fields of socks,
fruits, vegetables, massages,
Quranic advisors, reading glasses' anti-fogging agent wipes.

if it were winter for a while in Milwaukee
Oconomilwaukesha
let tomorrow be the day that we get away with murder
or at the very least try to sell overpriced
Lenny Dykstra and Gregg Jefferies baseball cards
to my fellow snot nose shit heads

much later, i ran into some money when i turned eighteen
went to Seven Mile Fair and got me an Indian head
gold plated cubic zirconia pinky ring
wore that mother fucker for years
finally drank beer there, too. just like dad and gramps
way too drunk became of me,
ay chihuahua, the sunlight.

the aroma of a porta-pottie stays with you
its septasis, its orange grit, and its chocolate

in the nineties Bruce Lee turned into Scarface
Scarface was everywhere
Scarface leather jackets, pocket calendars, vanity mirrors,
commemorative plates, posters, keychains, hair brushes,
christmas ornaments.
all
Scarface.

rubber dog poo hand buzzer squirty pistol
spiked brass knuckles, samurai sword, nazi flag, cheap sun dresses, army
helmets,
plastic baby faces ten cents each
just the face, hundreds of them, sound good, you want it or not?
vats of laundry detergent comprised of sugar, blue food coloring, and corn
starch

heroic Mexican lamps
heroic Mexican statuettes depicting
a distressed woman on mountain being saved by a mariachi
heroic Mexican snakeskin elf boots with the big ass curly toe

the love-o-meter, well placed just outside the restrooms, for a quarter
test the spirit of your penis and thrust
very germs all over that god damn thing
wanna check your blood pressure real quick?
that'll be a quarter,
chump.

corn niblets, pepper, and mayo in a styrofoam cup
bags of squeaky cheese curds
cool ranch dorito socks, yes, that's a blessing
Mexican bar mitzvah dresses
Michael Jordan's flu game t-shirts
Bob Marley's flu game t-shirts
anyone, if they had a flu game, you best believe they had a t-shirt

near the puppy hut
mystical cumbia playing on mini portable cd players
baseball caps with big horse head
embroidered on the side
HORSE, in big white letters
fantastic.

much later i would work third-shift at a nearby casino
and recognized one gambling regular as
the scary
cock-eyed ukrainian guy who'd exuberantly sell orange sunglasses
kids' bikes, knives, and old tv remotes.
lots of them
no batteries
no corresponding tv sets
just the remotes
probably for $1.15 each, or two for two, just for you,
pretty good deal, my friend, haha,
sound good? you want it or not?

an amish man and his wife selling something
i tried to be clear
i had no interest in their shit
Mexicans making the egg foo yung
and pork fried rice combo in a grand
and whirling blur

so many wallets so little time

now
you'll leave unable to remove
the smell of the freshly fried mini-donuts
outta your clothes and hair.

much later
as a man i played music there
one afternoon with my band
and through the sweat i could scarcely make out a black biker,
various orange skinned mixed martial arts honkie types,
and a Hmong family
dancing.
the father holding a cantaloupe underarm, can't say that i blame him.

at the end of our show
a little Mexican boy ran up
and handed me a dollar.
what a buddy, what a pal
full circle.

Goldmine; or, The Will and Testament of Gerald Pinski

DIANE REYNOLDS

A perspective on Milwaukee architecture via science fiction.

I've been told by pretty much everybody that I better put my will together. I don't know what they're all going on about, I look fine to me, but I guess there's no harm in it and maybe they know something I don't. Wouldn't be the first time.

You might think it's crazy of me to will all my everything to a girl I never met, but believe me, I know her better than you think. If you only saw her picture, you'd get it. She's got that classic look, with one of those dream faces you see that could never lie, even if it tried. She's got class, too, and it shows in everything she writes me. I'm the luckiest man around because it was her that got my wire by mistake. I told her where I'm from and she doesn't even care that we have eighty years between us.

Writing your own will feels like writing a letter to yourself. I'll probably find it ten years after I've forgotten about it and tear it up. Nothing personal though, nothing could ever change between Beatrice and I. It's just like that sometimes. Like looking at your own yearbook picture.

I wish I could meet her in some dark secret place, after the war, when Polynesian dreams are confessed inside the bar booth. Maybe they'll solve that one day and our love can be complete.

But all I can tell her is, "When they wire you my will, don't cry. Think of it like this: it's like you, you're there but you're already gone. But you're there. You lived your whole life and get to live it again through me. If you get sad, just remember, I haven't even been born yet."

I looked up her old neighborhood in some pictures at the library and I think I found her street. Bungalow houses lined up close to each other with a few housewives mingling on their lawns, young maple trees planted in front, one for each house, and it made me wonder which house was hers. They looked mostly alike. Actually I went there and it looks like that now, too, only more tired and crooked and a few houses have been replaced by empty grass lots that look like sudden sunny little parks, delightful until I remember someone's house used to be there. Hopefully not hers.

Up the block was a custard stand and I'm just certain her daddy must have taken her there because who could say "No" to little Beatrice?

There's a lot of custard stands around this town, crashed in all the neighborhoods like space ships, only now they've turned from selling hot dogs and cones to cigarettes and cell phones. People must not like ice cream like they used to. What I wanna know is where do fathers take their daughters after dinner. For a smoke?

Anyway, I started to think about her little girl wonder, skipping up the block early Friday nights watching the steeple-shaped roof of the custard stand call her like a church for ice cream. I just had to buy it for her. I bought it from 1956-1964, the most the law allows. And since it can only be eight years, I made it the years she might most treasure, when things were new and sweet and were first becoming her own. This is when you need ice cream the most. So I bought it for her and she'll have it one day soon, and when she finds out that it's all hers it will be a surprise that I had them put a treat on the menu just for her. I invented it for her. The Sweetheart Sundae. I hope I die on Saint Valentine's Day.

I keep my will sealed and certified on my dresser right where I can see it. I made it myself so no lawyer can say anything about it. I'm not supposed to tell yesterfolks any of this but I figure by the time anybody wises up to it I'll be sharing a beer with God so what can they do? The point is, every one of my investments I'm giving to Bea. I hope she can use them. All the rest won't do her any good. All the rest is bound to my world of the future, where people huff oxygen in airport lounges and toilet paper's made from plastic. It won't be her fault that she finds out about the future and the deal will already be done. They'll have to give it all to her. What good is a will otherwise?

Sometimes I start to think that maybe I belong with the good old boys of 1897, and I think it's a good thing they haven't yet figured out how to transport man or by now I would have left house and home. Just the other day this letter was delivered from one of my foremen through the wire. He doesn't know where I live, my broker Peter Barth is good with discretion like that, which brings me to my next point: make sure you can trust your agency.

Dear Sir,

As it has been some time that we have reported, you and I, mutually about the happenings both within the factory and throughout our great and growing city, I feel I can speak candidly with you on the basis of friends. I am not certain of all the goings on there to-day in Switzerland, though I'd like to mention some of our wonderful advances. I hope I can paint for you a vision of our progress, and hasten I say the future.

A new manufacturer seems to arrive with every fortnight, as the city is alive with production of every kind from steam engines to leather and on through to the bicycle, which has crazed the modern man to his every hour's whim. I might have advised your taking up the business if I had predicted the streetcar strike by the Milwaukee Electric Rail & Light company last year. An ethical man might wonder as to the nature of it all, however I was none the wiser, streetcars stopped like river boulders in a current of bicycles belling with solidarity under socialism, our city's most amiable virtue.

Just this year Kieckhefer Brothers Company and their stamping works has expanded the area of an entire city block to accommodate their 950 workmen to a height of five stories, the largest size ever planned. Close to its size, the Western Lime and Cement Co. is the largest producer of magnesian white lime in so I hear the world. Rail drives grain and iron through the center of the city. Tall and numerous stacks make from engine power a brick forest topped with a canopy of clouds. It is a mastery of nature that our nation's character has sought, and through it the frontier claimed.

The women of Milwaukee might I add are the spark between proprietary and leisure. They are well fed, joyously so through the sweetest city things, and move past as a florist's arms brimming with blooms in colors, shapes, smells that make a wonder of their being grown from nature. I have seen the fine ladies of Vienna, of Munich, and even with their fine dresses (and without) they hold no more charm than these, who are folly with ale and games of chance, knowing well saloon piano and the Gimbel's store, and all at once they are creatures of America.

As song and jubilee erupt this evening from countless halls, I look forward to your joining us when time affords you.

Humbly working for the benefit of our productivity, with all the fineness of life,

Solomon A. Dobrinz

And wouldn't you believe it, strikes sell bikes. I get my tips where I can. The bicycle factories have by now faded just the same as the tanneries and grain warehouses. I would have scarcely imagined them. They are faded or boarded or extracted like rotten teeth in the memory of a smile. It's a perfect business to live today.

Thank you Solomon Dobrinz. And thank you Peter Barth, who pulled from his tall metal cabinet the file on Telegram Cycle Manufacturing Company. The easiest and handsomest machine in the world, Peter said when he laid the spec out for me to see. It was a good Milwaukee building, cream brick with a cornice like pie crust. Broad open windows with striped cloth awnings. Or so the picture showed. There's a mess of condominiums there now. I bought it just the same, with a four-year clause. 1896-1900. Sometimes luck is waiting in the wings.

I remember my first investment. Some little creosote share from 1928. Public trade had just opened. That was before I met Peter Barth, my now long-trusted broker, and before I knew selling on Black Thursday had become restricted. Seems some MIT hotshot wrote a paper on it, that there's a doubling effect from withdrawing just before the crash. The government will believe anything these college boys write. I lost my ass on that deal.

A depression'll clear the mind of any great man from architect to engineer and zap him to that familiar place beneath his lofty dreams, that hard nut place we all know too well called survival.

The only dime I could turn in the thirties was on the invention of the electric razor. It's a good thing I found Peter Barth when I did. I got a tip to go to the docks, to the last terminal on Jones Island. It was down a service road between mountains of rock salt and freight ships that watched the city like gods. Flatly painted tin warehouses, silos, and bumper tug boats and cranes and discarded machinery claws, their shadows stretching on a maze made of stacked containers. It looked like nothing much. A purgatory maybe. So I found his office through the last door of the furthest warehouse, and wouldn't you know there he was.

He started in immediately, already standing up like he knew I was coming. Milwaukee is one of the nation's hottest markets, he told me, aside from St. Louis. I'm lucky to already live here, to get in on the ground level of this whole thing before everyone else does. I remember what he said, he said, "Anticipation is the hidden engine of progress."

He was the kind of man that looked like he must have cleared a grand that morning, that no amount of money could temper him. I bet he'd cut a hundred guys just like me into the game. That's the kind of man you want on your side in business. I knew he got it, that I could trust him.

He told me to keep sharp. The first ten years of this market is where all the money is, that any schmo with a library card can fake himself a pretty portfolio. He showed me his National Board of Timesourcing Trade certification stamp. No runaround about License Applied For.

His advice: factories are cheaper before Hitler because they use all sunlight. That Castro makes motorcycle sales hot. Buy the beauties and conceal them. Grand Victorians, ghosted signs, board them up, slap siding over them. There's a good chance they'll be here today waiting for you to flip them.

Beatrice wrote once that sometimes all people can do is make replicas of their memories. That replicas are the comfort of an aging world. But I told her that she was wrong, because now we can own the real thing.

It's a good town for business. The secrets of the past aren't given away. Not today. Your average guy can't see it for what was. He can't see through to the gold.

There are too many empty places, too elastic a stretch on the whole business of business. The suburbs are too vast. Too many buildings are left ripped open so we can see each brick that we might hold in our hand, and the lie of architecture is busted.

Your average man won't see it let alone believe.

I myself simply can't believe it sometimes, when I'm walking across some empty lot with all its weed and rubble, looking until I round the corner like there was never anything there, no empire of steel, no barley being changed to gold, just an empty open chance for stride, guns cocked.

The frontier is back again. We are American again. Decay today delivered me my fortune. And I took it. That's business.

Rebuild, Bubble, Rubble.

I should be driving, I say to myself. I could get in more territory that way.

Words from the Black Box

JOHN J. MUTTER, JR.

In the early 1970s, before I knew my wife, she had been visiting her two sisters in Milwaukee. They had gone to a garage sale and she purchased a small black box she thought might be ideal for storing hair curlers.

After she got the box home, she discovered that it was packed with correspondence. The letters went back to the year 1933, and through the years a few of the three-cent stamps had been cut off the envelopes.

Had she needed the box right away, she confessed she would have discarded the contents. In time, she met me. After showing the container to me and briefly looking at some of the letters, I told her I felt the material should be saved. That was in 1981. Twenty-eight years later, I have kept the box with all that is inside.

The wooden box was made by Geo. Burroughs & Sons, Manufacturers of Trunks & Leather Goods, 424-426 East Water Street, Milwaukee, and was made for the Avery Scale Company of North Milwaukee, Wisconsin. It appears to have been made for a particular scale company instrument. The box is seven-and-a-half inches tall, ten inches wide and six-and-a-half inches in depth. Its exterior is finished in black, split-hide leather with a speckled-fleck pattern. The box is protected from damage by eight ornate metal corner guards. With a tiny key, the container could be locked and on each side of the lock is a latch.

An inventory of the box disclosed 131 personal letters, four small photos, three yellowed newspaper clippings, a copy of the bylaws of the United Auto Workers of America—Local 364—receipts for coal, a business card from the Lincoln Scrap Iron Company in Milwaukee, and letters from several Milwaukee attorneys.

About 110 of the letters were written by a lady, or her daughter, who lived at 6303 West Blue Mound Road in Milwaukee. They were writing to their husband/father who was in the Wisconsin Prison System. The letters revealed that four of the parent's sons were incarcerated at the same time. All of the letters were saved by the father, as that's to whom they were addressed.

At first, in late 1933, the mother was writing to her husband in Spokane, Washington, and their son was close to being paroled from a Wisconsin prison. A newspaper clipping was sent about a $50,000 still that was seized in West Allis. It evidently was near the end of Prohibition as the article says, "The raid may be the last in Prohibition history in Milwaukee County."

It appears that soon after the father returned to Wisconsin from Washington, his son was paroled from the Wisconsin Prison System. Then, in early February of 1935, the father, the paroled son, and another son attempted to rob a filling station and were caught. The recently paroled son was shot by a Milwaukee police officer during the arrest, and survived the gunshot wound.

In March of 1935, the letters commence again and the father was in the Waupun State Prison. The letters have a round cachet mark, indicating the letter had been inspected by prison officials. Six letters were sent to him at Waupun and then he was transferred to the State Camp Farm at Lake Tomahawk, Wisconsin.

The mother describes a miserable existence in Milwaukee during the time of the Great Depression. She had all she could do to get enough money for the coal she needed to keep from freezing in Wisconsin's cold winter. The landlord raised the rent to $15 a month, even though the roof leaked terribly. She wanted to move, but couldn't find another place that would take her. On July 6, 1935, she writes: "The bank up the street here where we mail our letters, well that is a big fruit store now. It opened up the 29th of June."

Almost every day, there is someone pounding on her door wanting money that is owed. She has three cars belonging to family members, but she can't sell them. "Nobody wants them big gas eaters," she writes. Then she sells one of them for $11.

A newspaper article is enclosed in one of the letters from Blue Mound Road. It pertains to President Roosevelt's plan to share wealth in America—the start of Social Security taxes and old-age pensions.

She finally gets a job making dresses and, when paid, finds out that she wasn't getting thirty-three cents per hour, as she thought, but rather twenty-five cents. She takes home $6.41, for twenty-five hours worked. She is let go from the job and she searches to no avail for another. She doesn't want to go to the County for help, but breaks down and goes to get enough money for coal. Burning coal is a mess and she writes about having to clean the stovepipes almost every other day. They write to each other once a week. The letters are staggered, so they can answer each other's questions.

She also writes to her sons in prison. She always tells her husband not to worry about her, but the letters convey a great hardship. "This is the longest we been apart in nearly thirty years," the wife wrote. She usually signed off on her letters, "Love and Kisses and Loads of Luck." In one of his letters, he must have asked her why she always wished him "Loads of Luck?" She responded, "Because we never had any luck."

On April 17, 1936, the father is discharged from the Waupun State Prison. His parole papers are by order of the warden, who at that time was Oscar Lee. He returns to Blue Mound Road, but evidently the separation did not strengthen their marriage and they split up.

The father gets a job on a farm near Stoughton, Wisconsin, and begins to send money to his ex-wife, by order of the parole board. He gets to keep $1.50 per week for personal items he needs.

The last letter he received from his former wife is dated November 22, 1936. She writes: "Chickens here is fifteen and seventeen cents a pound. A goose is twenty-five cents a pound and so is ducks. Our basement sure is full of rats this winter. It's usually a race between Max (her dog) and the rats, to see who gets the eats."

In January of 1937, the father was working at the Lincoln Scrap Iron Company in Milwaukee, for fifty cents per hour. In September of 1937, he received a letter from his imprisoned son, who wrote, "Do you know it is the first one (letter) you have every wrote to me in my holl (sic) life and I am now thirty years old."

Words from the black box did not come from people with high educations. Their words at the time didn't seem to be valuable or important, but historically, it recorded a difficult time in our country.

Probably the most important aspect of the words from the black box, was the fact that they were saved; maybe unintentionally, but nevertheless saved by the father. It's a fair assessment that all the people involved in these personal letters are now deceased. Intended or not . . . the words of the Great Depression have lived on.

The Rippling Effect of Baron Walker

KEITH MCQUIRTER

"What more does Wisconsin need to know in order to find out I'm not a menace to society? That is actually the question I would like to know myself."
-Baron Walker

Baron Walker remembers the morning when he and his grandfather stood across from each other in the driveway of his grandfather's house. Both men kicking the tires of Baron's black 1989 Mercury Cougar LS, neither looked at the other the entire time they spoke.

"Whatever you're doing, just be careful, and be safe," Baron remembers his grandfather saying to him, as if he had intuitively read his mind.

A clean-cut, husky man, Baron's grandfather worked at the Patrick Cudahy pork processing plant in the suburbs of Milwaukee, where he'd earned a steady income for his family for many years. However, it was no secret that his grandson was drawn to the fast life of the streets. In spite of the deep love he felt toward Baron, the elder man couldn't bring himself to say what needed to be said. He kept looking at the ground.

"He said he basically wouldn't want to waste his time trying to tell me not to do what I already had my mind made out to do," Baron recalls.

His grandfather turned around and walked toward the house. Baron got in his car, and drove off.

It was the third of January, 1996. Baron was twenty-two.

Three weeks earlier, Baron had successfully robbed his first bank with a crew of seasoned bank robbers. By late afternoon, during the first snow of the year, they went on to complete what was Baron's second heist. But this time, they were not so lucky, and by evening's end, Baron would have to make the decision to surrender to the police or to lose his life to the twelve-gauge shotgun aimed dead-center at his chest.

In 2015, I came to Milwaukee seeking to understand why the 53206 ZIP code, which represented the north side of the city, was hailed by a UW-

Milwaukee study as the most incarcerated ZIP code in the nation. By age thirty-four, the study showed 62 percent of African American men in 53206 will have been imprisoned.

Many, including myself, would never have imagined a Milwaukee ZIP code outpacing the incarceration rates of ZIP codes in major cities like Detroit, Philadelphia, New Orleans, and St. Louis as the imprisonment capital of America for black men.

I first heard of Baron's story while researching online, and I discovered a 2014 audio series by WUWM 89.9 radio called "I Am More Than My Record." In it, Baron's wife Beverly Walker explained in thirty-four seconds how, despite his incarceration, Baron remained in the life of his family, as a husband and father of five, by telephone. She described how he tutored their children in the fifteen-minute blocks prison calls allow, and that he sent loads of cut-out coupons home so he could help financially.

I reached out to Beverly regarding a documentary I wanted to make to explore the people of 53206. Like so many people when approached by media, she was cautious—rightfully so. However, she agreed to have a conversation in public. A few days later, on a Saturday morning in August of 2015, I met Beverly at Sherman Perk Coffee Shop.

She was poised and graceful as she entered the colorful, quirky diner. Soon after we sat down, Baron called from Fox Lake Correctional Institution and joined in by speakerphone. We talked at length about the process of documentary filmmaking, and what it would entail if they were to get involved. As we parted, they said they needed to discuss everything as a family. Two days later Beverly called and said, "We're in."

Baron remained incarcerated. In 2015 he was serving year nineteen of the sixty-year sentence for the two armed bank robberies. (While nothing can reduce the gravity of his actions, thankfully, no one had been physically injured.) Baron had been sentenced prior to Wisconsin's adoption of its Truth in Sentencing Law. Such laws were enacted in forty-two states and the District of Columbia during the late 1990s and early 2000s. These laws came in several varieties, and under the Wisconsin version, inmates had to serve their full sentence—with no eligibility for parole. Yet Baron—along with approximately 3,000 other inmates in the state who were eligible for parole at that time—were also subject to this new law.

Baron, his family, and even the judge who sentenced him had expected that after serving 25 percent of that sixty-year sentence, he would be paroled. For pre-Truth in Sentencing prisoners like Baron, there was also presumptive mandatory release, at maximum, after an inmate had served two-thirds of his or her time.

However, nineteen years later, four years past the time he first became eligible for parole, Baron remained in prison. When I first met him in 2015, he was forty-one.

Even Baron was surprised by the person who first got him involved in robbing banks. It was a short, stocky college kid who was recognized for staying on the straight and narrow. Baron admired him for this; Baron was known for being intractable and had a street reputation.

At the time, Baron had been dealing drugs. As he puts it, "I was more devoted to the street, life was always living on the edge. Somebody was always telling me that I was supposed to be here, I was supposed to do this, and this way and that way. The streets seem to just accept."

Before his family moved to the 53206 ZIP code, Baron lived in the Hillside Housing Projects in one of the roughest areas of the city. He grew up a freckled-faced kid with red hair. He was known as "Red" to his family. In addition to the values he was being taught at home, he learned about life from the streets. He called the latter a miseducation, and a misunderstanding of what it was to be a man.

Still, Baron had a conscience. He had a churchgoing mother, and had been raised well. Growing up, he cites *The Autobiography of Malcolm X* as having influenced him tremendously. Reading it, he says, made him have "a love for my people, for my culture. So when I try to sell drugs it was contrary to that. It's a contrast, so I would do it for a while and I stopped."

While dealing, Baron said his intention was to "ride this thing, get this money, and open up a club." For a while, he recalls, he went legit:

"I had a job . . . I was working twelve hours a day and it was a pretty good job. I was bringing home like close to $700 every week. But it felt like I wasn't living, I didn't have a life. You know, when everybody else was doing something, going somewhere . . . I feel like I was just a slave to the job."

One day he got into an argument with his girlfriend at the time, and went to Capitol Court Mall to cool off. That's when he met that college kid—the one he admired. The one who would turn him on to robbing banks. He and his crew were younger than Baron. Prior to that time, Baron remembers of that kid:

"I was proud of him 'cause I see him and he was still going to school, and I was trying to sell drugs. I was telling him I'm glad that he was going somewhere better than me. He even turned me down [when I offered him money], and I was even proud of that because it felt like he didn't want no part of what was dark and dirty."

Baron recalls of that fateful encounter at the mall, "But now I see him and he got all this big old slab of chain, a coat, and some Timberlands." Curious about all that newfound polish and bling, Baron asked him, "What you doing?"

Baron joined them for his first robbery:

"It was hard, to be honest. I can tell you all that tough-guy gangster nonsense. But yeah, it was scary. It was scary because everything happens in a matter of seconds and because it's unpredictable. You enter into a place and you don't know what's going on, who is who, who may also have a weapon, and especially when you go in with a partner. To rob a bank, you don't know. You can't control him, his decision, his choice."

The first robbery, however, was flawless—and bloodless. A total success.

"I felt relieved afterwards. We felt like we had a sense of power," says Baron. "We had a lot of money and I went and got a car and bought some Christmas stuff for my family. We really started acting as though we were invincible."

His second bank robbery: a total disaster. Their haul from the first robbery had been $30,000. They didn't even need the money. Their team was in disagreement and disarray about robbing the next bank. Perhaps they had gotten overconfident—even greedy.

Baron says of the next heist, "We went there in a spur of the moment. We didn't have all our guns. It was really crazy. So we went in there and it seemed like it was, it seemed like out of control, really."

At that bank, "A lady had panicked. She just froze up, and I was starting to be concerned about whether or not my partner was gonna shoot her. So I had, I stood in front of her, and moved her out the way."

Baron grabbed the money from the register. It was booby trapped with dye packs and the repugnant smell of sulfur. When they got outside, Baron threw away the soiled money in the street and ran.

When they arrived at the house, an argument ensued between Baron and one of his partners about throwing the money away. Baron told him the money was no good, but his partner insisted on retrieving it despite Baron's insistent protest.

When his partner went down the block to retrieve the money, the police saw him pick something up, and surrounded him. Things escalated. Next thing, they were headed to the house where Baron was hiding.

While downstairs, the police interrogated Baron's friend, his friend's sister, and others, asking if there was anybody else at the house. Each time, they lied: No. The officers made their way up to the bedrooms upstairs, and there they found Baron in one of them, sitting on a bed. One officer pointed a twelve-gauge shotgun at his chest. Baron thought he was going to die.

As he was being arrested, that was the moment when "reality hit." Baron began to realize what this would mean for those he loved:

"I thought about my nieces. I thought about my grandfather. I thought about my son. I was supposed to get custody of my son the next day, the very next day . . . Everything just felt like it was over. I knew that this time is a wrap. I really messed up."

But here's what stayed with Baron most: When he left the house early that morning, the day of the robbery, he remembered that his mother, Jo Esther, was crying because she was concerned about the young lady he was dating at the time—his son's mother. His girlfriend had many issues, including drug abuse. Says Baron of his mother, "She's like, 'I'm trying to tell you that girl is no good. Leave her alone.'"

Baron digs deeper:

"I remember when I saw my mother crying on the porch. I had never seen her do that. And I was pulling out of the driveway, and I see her crying, and I stopped, I really stopped, and I looked at her. Then I remember thinking: 'Wow, she really needs this. She's really serious about what she's telling me about this girl. And I can see it . . . When I lost my mother, the last time I seen her in the world, she was standing on the porch crying, and I had made her cry.'"

After the botched robbery and court proceedings, he entered prison a troubled young man. And at first, he continued the behavior he'd learned on the streets. Eventually it led to him being accused, in one incident, of attempting to incite a riot, and despite his denials, it landed him in prolonged solitary confinement—also known as the Hole. He was segregated for five years, and sent to a super-maximum prison in Boscobel, Wisconsin, where there is only solitary confinement.

Shackled and assigned two guard escorts, he was given an hour a day of sunlight. While there, Baron thought about the fact that—if he never received parole—he'd do this until his release at eighty-one-years old. It was his mother's influence, steady and lifelong, that finally brought about change in Baron. His mother was an alcohol and drug counselor, and her love and instruction stayed with him long after that cell door slammed, giving him a belief in himself and the assurance that God would make a way for him.

Baron came to his own day of reckoning when he kept seeing the pain he was inflicting on the people that he loved. He decided then to step up and set the course of his own life: the sense of agency he'd been seeking as a young man (but misguidedly so) redirected and rekindled. Baron began to reach out for help with the hardship of his prolonged prison sentence, writing letters to his mother's church. He then wrote to more than twenty churches, in Milwaukee, Racine, and Kenosha.

He asked them to be a voice for him while in these inhumane conditions but also to be a counselor and guide, because that's where you go when you need help—you go to the church. He told them of his five-year confinement in the Hole, with its rubber-stamp interviews to justify further segregation. The powers that be felt he was still a danger to himself and others, and sent him back inside the Hole. In the end, a few churches promised prayers, but no involvement with the politics of prison. In the year 2000, Baron became a Muslim, and denounced his affiliation to any gangs.

Always told he was smart, Baron didn't realize that his natural ability to solve problems was actually intelligence. He just thought he always found a way to get solutions. In prison Baron found both solace and confidence in learning and absorbing everything available to him. He worked in food service as an assistant cook, a prep cook, and the lead cook in the bakery. The inspiration for his work ethic was his mother's words: "Do your best in the work you do, no matter what you do." He looked forward to going to work every morning, having a sense of purpose. He took the time to learn self-control, communication, and cooperation. He also increased in curiosity and confidence.

Baron's life-altering religious conversion became all-consuming, giving him those principles to live by that he'd previously lacked—even in spite of his mother's dedicated, ongoing efforts to give her son sage and loving counsel. What emerged was a man who thrived in any circumstance.

He learned the gift of hard work and built himself up, only to face the hardest challenge his life would bring him thus far: the murder of his mother by a man who had once been his friend. These were the darkest days of his life. This unexpected, brutal crime that took the life of the woman who was his rock was unimaginable. The grief was so intense, he couldn't move. He didn't want to see the sun, didn't want to wake up.

His supervisor in the food program at prison let him take the time to grieve, giving him an unheard-of two weeks off. He was so concerned about Baron that he allowed co-workers time off to comfort and support him as well. It was at this point that Baron and Beverly learned the complexity and power of the Department of Corrections and the parole board. It was in 2010 that Baron first went before the parole board. The parole liaison was both surprised and impressed at the accomplishments Baron presented to them. However, the board said they wanted further monitoring, and that Baron didn't do enough time, even though he had met all the requirements under his original sentencing. They gave him a thirty-month deferment. The next time he went to the parole board, they gave him an eighteen-month deferment. After that a twelve-month, then an eleven-month, and endorsed him to a minimum-security facility.

After the death of his mother, the parole denials led Baron to struggles with depression, and with each denial he struggled with despair, one time to the point where he stopped eating. Digging deep within himself once again, Baron decided not to give up and, with Beverly by his side, they fought back.

David Liners, the director of WISDOM, a Wisconsin grassroots faith-based organization that advocates and lobbies for prison reform, brought Beverly into several of its projects and eventually made her a spokesperson. She brought humanity and clarity to the subject of mass incarceration. She spoke for Baron, and elucidated injustices in the parole process for audiences. Despite her soft-spoken demeanor, Beverly is a commanding presence, and the more she spoke, the more people listened. Her charisma and effectiveness catapulted her into leadership. In 2014, Beverly spoke at the Fatherhood Initiative Summit in Milwaukee and to WUWM reporter Ann-Elise Henzl as part of her series, "I Am More Than My Record."

While Beverly and Baron were being seen in my movie, Beverly maintained a website that instructed people how to write support letters, not only for Baron, but concerning other cases and about parole and sentencing reform in general. The social impact campaign of *MILWAUKEE*

53206—although not designed to specifically advocate for Baron's release, but to raise awareness and promote discussion on the moral crisis of mass incarceration—prompted thousands of viewers to write letters about Baron's case. Milwaukee defense lawyer Craig Mastantuono saw the movie and took on Baron's case pro bono, which included sentencing modification work alongside the Milwaukee County District Attorney's office for cases like Baron's, caught between changing parole laws.

On August 16, 2018, Circuit Court Judge Mark Sanders modified Baron's sentence to time served on the first count, a stayed seven-year sentence with five years of probation for the second count, a re-entry program provided by nonprofit the Alma Center, and community service. The move to Truth in Sentencing was seen as a new factor and was counter to the original expectations of eventual parole. Even the bank manager who had testified at Baron's original hearing about being emotionally traumatized by the robbery was surprised to learn that, decades later, Baron was still in a cell.

The next day Baron officially became a free man.

The judge at Baron's original hearing had given him such a hefty sentence because she felt he was in need of correction and rehabilitation. He was a very different person then. During his prison stint, Baron reformed himself in earnest and took advantage of extensive educational and vocational training, while cultivating his spirituality in Islam. At the time of Baron's release, Judge Sanders noted of Baron's evolution over those more than two decades that he had demonstrated "on the whole, significantly improved character."

The 53206 ZIP code shares much in common with other US cities with high incarceration rates: hyper-segregation, deindustrialization, underfunded schools, expansive trauma, institutional racism, and all the trappings of poverty.

Flying in from my native New York City, I knew I'd find in Milwaukee what I'd also found parallel to those other cities with high incarceration rates: volunteer healers working tirelessly on the frontlines and faith-based organizations and nonprofits doing all they could to save lives and build a stronger community. What surprised me as I began production was the widespread interest in the film's subject matter, and both the support of Milwaukee itself, and the documentary's ultimate impact there.

In the last few years, the United States has been slowly waking up to the moral crisis it faces in its criminal justice system. There are plenty of resources that deeply probe the causes of mass incarceration, but there is little that explores the human toll of its devastation, especially in communities of color. Like a stone thrown into water, Baron and Beverly's story embodies the outward ripple effects of the mass incarceration crisis in Milwaukee and for families and communities like theirs across the nation. Nevertheless, Beverly and Baron fought hard to keep their family bonds not just intact, but active, vibrant, and muscular.

There is a troubling national trend of parole boards vanishing, due to policy changes in sentencing. In Wisconsin, where Truth in Sentencing was in enacted in 1998, it virtually abolished the state's parole board for those sentenced after the new law. For the thousands of inmates sentenced under the old law, the picture is still bleak. The parole board, which, until 2018, was comprised of a committee of members, has been reduced to one person who decides the fates of all the state's old law parole-eligible inmates, and who, like in Baron's case, as a matter of practice, are routinely denied despite meeting their requirements. This consolidation of power, an anemic, diluted version of what is supposed to represent justice, can be demoralizing for the incarcerated. Further, unlike Baron, their voices are still largely silent. There are no cameras, no media, and no journalists looking at their cases.

It is in Baron and Beverly's freedom that there may be a sign of hope in Wisconsin. Baron Walker is one example of how a man transformed himself from his misguided years and youthful indiscretions to a man who is fully accountable and responsible for his past and who seeks to better himself, the lives of his family, and his community. If we are going to have significant reform in our criminal justice system, it will require a deep change in how our nation's prisons rehabilitate and give our parole-eligible offenders (particularly those who were formerly violent) a second chance in life.

It's stories like that of the Walkers that help to humanize incarceration. In opening up their lives as a family to the world, they show the real story behind the white paper statistics, and help those of us who want to see justice done alchemize empathy into action. With the nation grappling with a moral crisis facing the current state of incarceration in America, it is my fervent hope more people will lend their voices for justice, so that in time, change will come.

Reverse Commute

VALERIE VALENTINE

Reverse commuting to Waukesha,
against the lanes of eastbounds going downtown daily,
leaping lanes
past Miller Park felt
like a salmon ramming upstream in spring.

One day the flow slowed: road construction
—the push of progress's pressure
built frustration into the endeavor;
but work is meaningful money
when you owe your first mortgage.

Going home (others went out as I came in)
94 to 43, slicing our city into hemispheres, like
the Milwaukee River,
sparkling down by a candycane lane of condos,
churned mud sliding, Wonka's chocolate flowage.

The dog would live for those afterwork swims,
but the vets blamed river gunk for infecting her lungs:
blasto fungus eventually ate her, she lost an eye.

We'd clean up the river every year, yet it continued to
churn up chunks, trash from eras gone by,
requiring sisyphean spring cleaning.

And the riverkeepers still rally the troops
for the job that's never done,
reversing a garbage tide with community pride.

Mandela's Milwaukee

MICHAEL PERRY

By now Mandela Barnes is the lieutenant governor of Wisconsin. Or he isn't. Last I saw him he was in Milwaukee eating chicken wings. This is a mild protein irony as our meeting was precipitated by beef.

Where I come from, what you did is you *heard* about Milwaukee. Heard about beer, beer, beer. Heard about the Brewers and Bucks, and once a year watched an away-home Packers game cut by the dirt of County Stadium. Heard the buildings were tall, the rest a sprawl. Heard getting there was an Indy 500 snarl. Maybe—*maybe*—heard about the lakefront or the Pfister, but mostly heard about all them places you didn't dare go. Heard about all the guns and shooting. And not the kinda guns and shooting stamped for approval by an NRA decal. We heard they killed each other for basketball sneakers. Heard they would not so much as raise a finger toward their bootstraps. *They, they, they*, we *heard, heard, heard*. And later, when we heard about all the crack and how they were smoking it up, we leaned against our pickup trucks, the beds rattling with empties, and nodded knowingly over all the trouble with a place we'd never been.

I am daily grateful to be *of* and *from* rural Wisconsin. Of a place where the local country music oldies station still runs listener-submitted liners the likes of, "If you've ever used binder twine for a belt . . . *yer one of us.*" Or, "If your first date involved a two-for-one coupon . . . *yer one of us.*" Or, "If you've ever gone to a funeral just to check out the buffet . . . *yer one of us.*" I wrote those last two, and when I heard them emanate from my pickup truck radio it was like I won a Pulitzer *and* a Grammy.

One day while traveling to perform at Lake Superior Big Top Chautauqua (up there by Bayfield—about as northern Wisco as you can go) I drove past a sign in Trego. That night I worked it into the act: "If you live within fifty miles of a billboard advertising a beef jerky outlet store . . . *yer one of us.*" It got a good laugh, which I figured it would, as I pictured all us camo-cap roughnecks gnawing on beef sticks between trips to the deer stand in the land of Jack Link's. Even as I bathed in the chuckles, there was to be found on the floor of my van an empty bag of Original Flavor.

I polished the billboard bit over the course of several jobs north of Highway Eight. Each time I took the laughter as an endorsement of my pinpoint powers of colloquial observation. Self-congratulations swelled my head. Then one day, while checking politics on Twitter (which is like checking your oil during a demolition derby) I caught a Mandela Barnes tweet: "I'm late to the party here, but there's a beef jerky outlet twenty minutes outside of Milwaukee. One of the most emblematic things of this state."

In that instant I realized the perception upon which I built my joke was incomplete, inaccurate, and spoke poorly to my powers of observation. I've criss-crossed Wisconsin for years, past Mandela Barnes's jerky billboard and others, but because I'd so presumptively geo-tagged the idea in terms of *here* and *there*, of *us* and *them*, I'd succumbed to tunnel vision. I'd nailed a tiny frame over a big picture.

▲▲▲

I was invited by the publication you are now reading to compose a northerner's impressions of Milwaukee, but there has been quite enough of that. Instead, I arranged a phone call with Mandela Barnes. A Democrat and former state representative, he's now running for the gubernatorial equivalent of vice president. It's July, and he has yet to win the primary. He's out there "Barnes-storming," or at least that's what I'd call it if any of you high-dollar, dark-money types want to put my brilliance on retainer. Our conversation is halting, just as you might expect between two people who have never met, one of whom has been handed his phone by a campaign aide to take non-campaign questions.

I begin by referring to his beef jerky outlet tweet. "Everywhere you go!" he says. "It's just an odd thing to see. There are cheese outlet signs everywhere, too. We're unique in that way."

Barnes tells me he was born in "a very challenging part of the city." Then he rephrases. "A very challenging part of the *state*." The distinction is a matter of inclusion. "It definitely feels like bigger cities are left out of the midwest conversation or the midwest identity in general," says Barnes.

I mention Roxane Gay referencing (in a tweet, natch) her exhaustion over journalists who assume all Midwesterners are white, and Barnes agrees. "They paint the Midwest with a very rural brush that is more homogeneous than it actually is."

Barnes is third-generation Milwaukee. His grandfather served in World War II, then came to the city to raise his family. "Like so many other people in that generation or even before him, he was able to work, family-sustaining jobs in a factory town, a very industrial city," says Barnes. "[Today] you have the cultural piece without the economic piece. We're in a place where it feels like we're tryin' to find a new identity."

I ask Barnes: If you had one day to show me Milwaukee, where would we go? "Back in 2015 we had an exchange group from the Philippines," he says. "It was a little too cold to go down by the lake, but we went downtown, we went to the Lakefront Brewery, we did a fish fry, just kind of drove around the different neighborhoods. Showed them the diversity. It's easy to think of Milwaukee as this homogeneous place, but it is absolutely not. It takes going down Sixteenth Street viaduct, it takes going to the East Side of the city, to the northwest side of the city, to the near South Side of the city . . ." The answer in his answer is you can't show a place, you have to come to know it. The whole "Top Five Spots" trope is just another version of Tiny Frame Syndrome. Conversation is more important than itinerary.

In the weeks following our phone conversation, Barnes won the primary and his schedule blew up accordingly. I had entertained visions of us touring "his" Milwaukee, but over the course of numerous emails, it became clear our respective logistics wouldn't support it. When my own schedule put me just outside Milwaukee for a few hours, I arranged to meet him for a campaign event in Milwaukee at the YWCA on Doctor Martin Luther King Junior Drive. It was a low-key affair. He engaged in light sparring with some Libertarians (the Republicans did not attend) but by and large it was a gathering of neighbors trying to do better for, and by, their neighbors. Afterward Barnes and I retired to a pub to visit until those chicken wings came.

We took another stab at establishing Milwaukee's Five Top Stops, but quickly abandoned it as a contrivance. Instead, we talked about what made a neighborhood a neighborhood. "When we moved from where we were to where my Dad is now, we were one of the only black families there.

So it was much different than where I was born, where I grew up, where I spent the early years of my life. Stark contrast. But either place, my Dad was *intentionally* neighborly. He still is. Dad knew everybody in the old neighborhood, everybody still knows him if he shows up there today. He walks every day, says hi, speaks to everybody. I think neighborly is more individualized than we think."

The wings arrive. I am about to turn off my recorder and let Barnes eat, but he has one more story. "I was in Waupaca campaigning," he says. "This woman said, 'You're not from the *bad part*, are you?' I was like, 'What?!?' She said, 'I don't know, I've heard so many things . . .' I said, 'You should just come on down to Milwaukee. We'll hang out.' She said, "I don't know . . .' She was super hesitant. Like she didn't ever want to come here."

"Where would you take her?" I ask.

He waves at Milwaukee all around him.

"Anywhere, really."

The *"yer one of us"* catchphrase is a variation on the old Jeff Foxworthy *"You might be a redneck if . . ."* bit, although I like to think our version is gentler and more inclusive. More neighborly. But I also know how long it took me to recognize Doctor Martin Luther King Junior Drive in Milwaukee as part of the Heartland.

If elected lieutenant governor, will Barnes be extended *"yer one of us"* privileges statewide? Right around the time we met, his incumbent opponent took to Twitter declaring that Barnes believed in kneeling during the national anthem. "In fact," she wrote, "Wisconsin neighbors have told me that they have seen him do exactly that."

It was a pernicious little move, handing off to the neighbors. The secondhand gossipy tone of it. Reporting what you *heard, heard, heard.*

Whispers, slithering through white picket fences.

Author's note: in January 2019, Mandela Barnes was sworn in as Lieutenant Governor, along with his gubernatorial running mate, Tony Evers. The duo defeated GOP incumbent Gov. Scott Walker and Lt. Gov. Rebecca Kleefisch for a four-year term.

ACKNOWLEDGMENTS

First, for the kindness and patience, thanks to my wife, Jessica Franklin and, because she'd insist, our cats, Esmeralda, Luna, and Phantom.

The anthology is primarily the work of other people. But for my part I'd like to especially thank some of those people who directly helped me in such creative ways that it felt more like friendship than work: Todd Lazarski, Paloma Chavez, Nina and Jeff Lynne, D. S. White, Teresa Craze, Rashidah Butler-Jackson, David W. Bailey and Ana Vafai, Rebecca Chriske, Angie West, Jeremy Podolski, Steph Crosley, Stacey Stewartson at Reginald Baylor Studio, Sharon McGowan, Kennita Hickman and Megan McGee, Sylvia Desrochers with No Studios, Elmer Moore, Abraham Toro, Peter and Nick Woods, and Nora Normandy and Bert Ulrich at NASA.

Most of all, thank you to Belt Publishing, especially Martha Bayne and Anne Trubek, who believe in Milwaukee and in the greater voice of our region; to everyone who put their heart into a submission that showed me more visions of our city than could fit into print (here, anyway); and to the incredible roster of writers in this anthology: talented, compassionate and distinct, one and all . . . together, you've helped to share important views of Milwaukee with the world.

CONTRIBUTORS

Sammy Arechar is a stand-up comedian originally from Milwaukee. He has been featured on MTV and is the official spokesperson for Chicken Cobb Salad.

Having earned a BA from the University of Chicago, and a JD from the University of Wisconsin Law School, **Frances Assa** prosecuted employment discrimination cases in Milwaukee and elsewhere for the US Equal Employment Opportunity Commission for twenty-one years. Since retiring, she has had essays and articles published in literary journals and authored a chapter in the book *Nabokov's Women*. She has just completed a book entitled *Liberal Imaginations* about common threads in the lives and works of H. G. Wells, Edmund Wilson, Vladimir Nabokov, and Graham Greene in the context of twentieth-century history.

Reginald Baylor is the founder and creative director of Reginald Baylor Studio, a brand that is obsessed with the creative industry in Milwaukee and beyond. While the studio originally began with a focus on painting, it has consistently worked within a wide variety of media and produces everything from community artwork and public murals to branded coloring books and personal accessories. Most recently, Baylor has been producing fabricated items in order to explore the impact of design and commodification on the creative lifestyle.

Dug Belan used to be an interesting person with loads of friends, but is doing much better now. He currently lives in the wonderful state of Wisconsin.

Sue Blaustein retired in 2016 after twenty-five years as a food safety inspector for the Milwaukee Health Department. Her work has appeared in *Blue Fifth Review, Stickman Review, Kudzu Review* and other publications. She recently published her book, *In the Field, Autobiography of an Inspector*. Please see sueblaustein.com for publication links and details.

Mark Borchardt is a playwright who lives a full life in Milwaukee. He's written, produced, and directed radio dramas as well. In 2017 he had plays produced/read for Village Playhouse in Milwaukee and Samuel French in Los Angeles for their festivals. And in 2018 his play, *Coffee Shop*, won the Audience Award for best script at the Village Playhouse.

James E. Causey is an award-winning editorial columnist, special projects reporter, and contributing editor for the *Milwaukee Journal Sentinel*. James has spent more than twenty-five years as a professional journalist since becoming the first and the youngest African American high school intern at the *Milwaukee Sentinel* at age fifteen. He worked for the paper every summer until completing high school and then became a night cops' reporter while studying journalism at Marquette University where he later received his bachelor's degree. James continued his education at Cardinal Stritch University, and received his MBA in 2002. In 2008, Causey received a Nieman Fellowship from Harvard University. During his time there, he studied the effects of hip-hop music on urban youth.

He uses his skill set to highlight the issues that impact the urban community and he speaks for those who don't have a platform or a voice. Milwaukee Inner-city Congregations Allied for Hope (MICAH) recognized James in 2014 with the "To Do What is Just" Award for his outstanding work on the mass incarceration crisis of black men. Causey also received a NABJ award in 2014 for his business piece, "Buying Black." Causey is an active member of NABJ, former president of the Wisconsin Black Media Association, and member of Phi Beta Sigma Inc. He was also awarded the 2013 Morse-Marshall alumni of the year. Along with his professional accomplishments, Causey is a self-published author of two fiction books, *The Twist* and *Twisted*. Causey is currently working on his third book, non-fiction, titled *Warrior: The Untold Story of Gerald McClellan*.

Luke Chappelle is an artist who lives in Milwaukee with his dog and cat. His work employs psychedelia, minimalism, and surrealism to explore themes of transcendence, wilderness, and mystery. Vivid colors, opulent textures, and fluid linework balance with uncommon materials and methods to create stunning and unique works of primitivistic futurism.

Cover artist **Paloma Chavez** is a graphic designer and freelance screen printer whose projects have taken her from the Olympics in Rio de Janeiro to the NFL series in Mexico City to poster designs for the likes of David Byrne, Leon Russell, and Jim Gaffigan. A native of Guadalajara, Mexico, she currently lives in Milwaukee with her family, where she precariously balances a love of working out and pizza.

Ching-In Chen is the author of "The Heart's Traffic" and "recombinant," winner of the 2018 Lambda Literary Award for Transgender Poetry. Chen is also the co-editor of *The Revolution Starts at Home: Confronting Intimate Violence Within Activist Communities* and *Here Is a Pen: an Anthology of West Coast Kundiman Poets*. A poetry editor of the *Texas Review*, they teach creative writing at Sam Houston State University. More at chinginchen.com

Jan Chronister now lives and writes in the woods near Maple, Wisconsin, but grew up near woods close to Greenfield Park. She rode a bus daily to UW-Milwaukee where she graduated with a degree in English.

Matt Cook is the author of five books of poetry: *In the Small of My Backyard, Eavesdrop Soup, The Unreasonable Slug, Proving Nothing to Anyone*, and, most recently, *Irksome Particulars*. His work has been anthologized in *Aloud: Voices from the Nuyorican Poet's Café, The United States of Poetry*, and in Garrison Keillor's *Good Poems, American Places*. He was Milwaukee's Poet Laureate from 2015 to 2017.

Toni Edwards lives with her family in Milwaukee's Havenwoods neighborhood.

Jabril Faraj was born in Pasedena, California, before relocating at the tender age of two months to Milwaukee. His childhood was spent reading and running around in the Riverwest neighborhood of northeastern Milwaukee where he also attended Milwaukee Public Schools' Riverside University High School. He left Milwaukee to attend the Medill School of Journalism at Northwestern University, graduating in early 2010. After graduation, Jabril returned to Milwaukee, falling back in love with the city he grew up in. He was drawn back toward writing as a vessel for self-expression and self-care. Jabril published his first book, *Taking Stock*, a sixty-three-poem anthology, in January 2018.

Vianca Iliana Fuster is a Puerto Rican journalist in the first year of her career. She works as a multimedia producer at 88Nine Radio Milwaukee, producing both audio and video stories for on-air play and social media platforms. Vianca was born and raised on the South Side of Milwaukee in the Walker's Point neighborhood, graduated from Riverside University High School in 2013, and earned her bachelor's in journalism, advertising, and media studies from UW-Milwaukee in 2018. Vianca is twenty-three years old.

After service in county government as a career choice, **Jude Genereaux** retired as Door County's first county administrator in 2006. A life-changing attendance in a writing workshop in 1994 brought her to meet the love of her life, Norbert Blei, and to recognize her own role as a writer. Milwaukee became their favorite place of retreat and comfort during their life together, until Blei's too early death in 2013. An award winning poet, Jude's work has been published by Cross+Roads Press, Wisconsin Academy, *Hummingbird*, and a solid number of small press and newspapers. She has three chapbooks of essays and poetry, and writes a column for the *Rice Lake Chronotype*.

Ken Germanson is president emeritus of the Wisconsin Labor History Society after serving as its president from 1991 until 2009. He was a labor union official for more than thirty years after beginning his career as a newspaper reporter for several midwestern publications. After his retirement in 1992, he was employed some twenty-four years for a community-based organization that served Milwaukee's low-income families.

Mariella Godinez Munoz is a mother of two. She is a local journalist who has worked in the Milwaukee media industry for more than fifteen years. She said Milwaukee has given her the greatest opportunities in life and allowed her to volunteer and educate those in her community.

Brent Gohde was born in Wauwatosa and has resided for his entire life in the 414 area code. He founded the Cedar Block Arts Collaborative in 2005, which is behind a dozen events in partnership with the Milwaukee Art Museum, Milwaukee Film, and Alverno Presents. Brent writes marketing content weekdays from 9:00-5:00, and spends the rest of his waking hours on fiction, essays, and poems. Stay tuned for more from Cedar Block.

John Gorman is a writer from Dayton, Ohio, who lives on the South Side of Milwaukee with his wife and their two young boys. His work has been published by *CinemaBlend*, *Overthinking It*, the *Classical*, *Bearded Gentlemen Music*, and several other outlets whose archives have been permanently deleted from the internet. Get in touch with him on Twitter @GormanJP.

Callen Harty is the author of *My Queer Life*, a collection of writings on living a queer life, *Empty Playground: A Survivor's Story*, and *Invisible Boy*. In addition, he is the author of twenty-four plays, nearly 200 blog posts, and he has published poems, articles, and essays.

Fefe Jaber was born and raised on the South Side of Milwaukee to a big Palestinian family. She's currently a Pre-Law third-year year student at DePaul University, majoring in political science and journalism with a minor in economics. After undergrad, she plans to attend law school and one day give back to Milwaukee, the city that has given her everything.

Bryan Johnston is a second-year resident in family medicine at the Medical College of Wisconsin. He grew up in Olympia, Washington, and has lived in Milwaukee for six years. He finds that practicing medicine and writing both inform each other, and both help him to get closer to humanity.

Pardeep Kaleka is the eldest son of Satwant Singh Kaleka—the president of the Sikh Temple of Wisconsin, who was gunned down during the attacks of August 5, 2012. Pardeep grew up in Milwaukee and graduated from Marquette University. A former Milwaukee police officer, Pardeep is currently a teacher in the inner city and a leader of Serve 2 Unite, a nonprofit that battles against racism, bigotry, and ignorance.

Dasha Kelly is a writer, performer, and creative change agent who seeks to amplify community connections by facilitating discussions about topics, like race and class, that often divide communities. She utilizes the breadth of her talents and experiences to reach audiences ranging from college campuses to correctional institutions. She has released four spoken-word recordings, written two novels, and appeared on HBO's *Russell Simmons Presents Def Poetry Jam*. She has twice been a finalist for Poet Laureate of Wisconsin and was named Artist of the Year by the City of Milwaukee. She also founded Still Waters Collective, a network for storytellers and language enthusiasts. Kelly was the first artist-in-residence invited to Lebanon's Rafiki Hariri University for a partnership with the American University of Beirut. She has traveled as a US Embassy Arts Envoy to Botswana and the Island of Mauritius.

Justin Kern is a nonprofit communications person and nonfiction writer who lives in Milwaukee with his wife and cats. His words have been published in two other Belt anthologies as well as *Utne Reader, Great Lakes Review, Buffalo Spree, Forth, Milwaukee Record, Longshot Island, Wanderlust Journal,* and in daily newspapers in Wisconsin and western New York. He's a proud uncle, lifelong amateur musician, and decent horseshoe pitcher. His first book— tentatively titled *Conniving for Nothing*—will be out eventually.

A proud Milwaukeean, **Jim Kogutkiewicz** learned the ins and outs of Waukesha County commuting there for several years while working as a newspaper reporter and editor. He now stays east of 124th Street almost exclusively, working in the city's advertising industry. He lives in Shorewood, which his mother labeled "the ritzy side of town."

Catherine Lanser is a writer from Madison who grew up on the shores of Lake Michigan. She has lived in the Midwest her whole life and writes essays and narrative nonfiction about her life and growing up as the baby of a family of nine children. She is looking for a home for her first full-length memoir about how she found her place in her family, told through the lens of her brain tumor and her father's stroke.

Todd Lazarski is the author of the novels *Make the Road by Walking* (Red Giant Books, 2016), and *Spend It All* (Red Giant Books, 2019). His overwritten musings on food have appeared in *Eater*, *Paste*, and can most often be found in the *Shepherd Express*. He lives with his wife, the graphic artist Paloma Chavez, their daughter, Nina, and cat, Chencho, on Milwaukee's South Side, a stone's throw from both the world's best bánh mì and a vacant field that General Mitchell Airport has designated as the crash spot for downbound airplanes.

Laura Richard Marshall is a lifestyle designer and writer living in Milwaukee's Sherman Park neighborhood. She loves writing and living authentic stories of beautiful people and places made fully alive and appreciated. Laura and her husband are raising four daughters in a house that was once full of mold and raccoons and is now a beautifully restored home on one of Sherman Park's historic blocks.

Freesia McKee is author of the chapbook, *How Distant the City* (Headmistress Press, 2017). Her words have appeared in *cream city review*, the *Feminist Wire*, *Painted Bride Quarterly*, *Gertrude*, *Rogue Agent*, and *Huffington Post*. Freesia's poetry is forthcoming in *CALYX* and *Sinister Wisdom*.

Keith McQuirter is an award-winning producer and director with credits in TV documentary, new media, and commercials. His documentary, *MILWAUKEE 53206*, won the Grand Jury Prize for Best Feature Documentary at the 2017 Urbanworld Film Festival and won the National

Council on Crime and Delinquency's 2017 Media for a Just Society Award. Keith also co-produced the five-part Peabody Award winning and prime-time Emmy-nominated docu-series *Brick City* for the Sundance Channel. Having worked a number of years as an executive producer in advertising, Keith produced commercials for national and international brands in entertainment, apparel, beauty, food, and consumer products. Keith studied film and television production at New York University Tisch School of the Arts where he was awarded the Martin Scorsese Young Filmmaker Award. He also studied directing at the National Theater Institute. His production company, Decoder Media, is based in New York City.

Edgar Mendez is a beat reporter for the *Milwaukee Neighborhood News Service* and he grew up on Milwaukee's South Side, where he still lives. Mendez won a regional Edward R. Murrow Award and Milwaukee Press Club Gold Award for his reporting on South Side taverns.

John J. Mutter, Jr., was born in Racine in 1943. His father's family lived in Cudahy and his mother's family are from South Milwaukee. He has lived in the Shawano, Wisconsin, area since 1949.

Cheryl Nenn is the riverkeeper for Milwaukee Riverkeeper, a science-based advocacy organization that works for swimmable, fishable rivers throughout the Milwaukee River Basin. Cheryl has a BS in biology from the University of Illinois at Urbana-Champaign and an MS in Natural Resource Ecology and Management from the University of Michigan. Prior to working with Milwaukee Riverkeeper, Cheryl has worked with the US Forest Service, US Peace Corps, the City of New York Natural Resources Group, the Michigan Department of Natural Resources/Department of Agriculture, and an environmental consulting firm specializing in natural area management and water quality issues.

Elizabeth Harmatys Park is a Wisconsin native, a sociologist, and a peace and prison volunteer. Her poetry has been published in journals and in the Wisconsin Poetry calendar. She is the past recipient of the Jade Ring First Prize in poetry awarded by the Wisconsin Writers Association.

Michael Perry is a humorist, songwriter, playwright, and author of several books including *Population 485* and *The Jesus Cow*. He and his family live in rural Wisconsin. He can be found online at sneezingcow.com.

Zack Pieper is a poet, performer, singer, scribbler, and recording artist. He has lived in Milwaukee for eighteen years. He is the co-founder of the Activities Archive, an ongoing web-based compendium of recorded ephemera spanning several decades, with a focus on certain Milwaukee collaborators.

Diane Reynolds is living and working in Milwaukee, calling it a most recent home of twelve years. Currently she's being drawn, quartered, and sent to the four corners of her world: architecture, writing, photography, and dinner.

Tia Richardson is a full-time community mural artist. She partners with diverse groups of people to create vibrant murals that reflect their communities. Her work has been covered in news and film, which can be viewed at cosmic-butterfly.com.

Alex Rose was born in 1993 and she is an emerging artist based in Milwaukee. She completed a BFA in photography from the Milwaukee Institute of Art and Design in 2015. Her poem, "Where love is love is love," takes place in and around Lakeshore State Park.

Henry Schwartz is the co-founder and president of MobCraft Beer, the world's first crowdsourced brewery. He's a seasoned world traveler who had his entrepreneurial beginnings selling skateboards in Colorado.

Lauren Sieben is a writer in Milwaukee. Her reporting and essays have appeared in the *Washington Post*, the *Guardian, Racked, Midwest Living* and *Milwaukee Magazine*, among other outlets.

Rachel Seis is a writer and magazine editor based in Milwaukee's Bay View neighborhood. A resident of Milwaukee since 2008, she's continually surprised by the charm and curiosities she's stumbled upon while exploring her beloved adopted hometown.

Cris Siqueira is a multimedia artist who started her career at MTV Brazil. She holds master's degrees in film and history from UW-Milwaukee and her experimental short films have been shown in festivals worldwide.

Carl A. Swanson explores and writes about his adopted hometown. His latest book, *Lost Milwaukee*, was published in 2018 by The History Press. He lives in Milwaukee's Riverwest neighborhood with his wife, three children, and two cats.

Harvey Taylor is a founding member of the thirty-plus-year Earth Poets and Musicians performance ensemble. He's also a peace and justice activist, avid gardener, poet, songwriter, composer, CD/video producer, and photographer, who particularly enjoys gigging with his partner, Susie Krause, in Susie and Harvey's Adventures In Song. More at harveytaylor. net and Facebook.

Robert Earl Thomas was born in Oshkosh, Wisconsin, in 1977. For the first six years of his life he and parents Roger and Carol Thomas lived in northern Wisconsin (in and around the Bad River Reservation). At the age of seven his parents moved to Milwaukee where he has lived ever since.

Paige Towers is a creative and freelance writer who earned her BA from the University of Iowa and her MFA from Emerson College. She currently lives in the Riverwest neighborhood of Milwaukee and is at work on a book of essays about sound. Her writing has appeared in the *Harvard Review*, the *Baltimore Review*, *McSweeney's*, *Midwestern Gothic*, *Prime Number*, and many other publications.

Valerie Valentine is an editor and writer in Wisconsin. Her favorite part about Milwaukee is the water: Great Lake Michigan and the rivers. She lived in Riverwest for five years and now commutes to Milwaukee from Tichigan.

Maa Vue is a Hmong singer and songwriter based in Weston, Wisconsin. In February 2018, she was named president of her recording label, Yellow Diamond Records. Maa is best known for her hit single, "Nyob Ua Ke" ("Stay Together"), whose music video has accumulated over four million views on YouTube since its release in late 2013. Her follow-up album, "Sij Hawm" ("Time"), released in July 2016, included the hits "Rov Pom Koj Dua" ("See You Again," feat. David Yang) and "Txiv Lub Xim Xaus" ("Father's Violin"). In just one year of its release, her music video for "Rov Pom Koj Dua" accumulated over four million views.

Matt Wild is the co-founder and co-editor of Milwaukee Record, an arts and entertainment site covering the greater Milwaukee area and parts of Dodge County. He lives on Milwaukee's East Side.

Joanne Williams has spent her life in media, including stints as a reporter for Milwaukee's WTMJ and Chicago's WGN, and later on with award-winning years at Milwaukee's FOX6 and as host of Milwaukee Public Television's *Black Nouveau*. She was a regional director on the board of the National Association of Black Journalists, a founding member of the Wisconsin Black Media Association, and is a member of the Milwaukee Press Club Hall of Fame. In her "retirement," Joanne has worked with United Way of Greater Milwaukee and Waukesha County and has become associated with Milwaukee Film as an independent documentary filmmaker, currently producing, writing and directing *Kaukauna and King: 50 Years Later*.